A GARDENER IN THE WASTELAND

Jotiba Phule's Fight for Liberty

based on the 1873 work

SLAVERY.

(IN THE CIVILISED BRITISH GOVERNMENT UNDER THE CLOAK OF BRAHMANISM)

EXPOSED BY

JOTIRAO GOVINDRAW FULE

(ब्राह्मणी धर्माच्या आडपडद्यांत)

गुलामगिरी.

(सुधारल्या इंग्लिश राज्यांत.)

हें लहानसें पुस्तक

जोतीराव गोविंदराव फुले

यांनीं

लोक हितार्थ केलें

तें

पुणें येथें "पुना सिटी प्रेस" छापखान्यांत छापलें.

किंमत १२ आणे

गरीब शूद्रादिअतिशूद्रांस ६ आणे

[१८७३ मध्यें प्रकाशित झालेल्या प्रथमावृत्तीतील मुखपृष्ठाचें यथामूळ मुद्रण]

A Gardener in the Wasteland: Jotiba Phule's Fight for Liberty

Story: Srividya Natarajan

Art: Aparajita Ninan

First published in December 2011, reprinted 2018, 2020, 2022

ISBN 9788189059460

Typeset in Joti font, designed by Aparajita Ninan

Published by Navayana Publishing

155, Second Floor, Shahpur Jat, New Delhi 110049

www.navayana.org

Printed and bound by Sanjiv Palliwal, New Delhi

A GARDENER IN THE WASTELAND

Jotiba Phule's Fight for Liberty

STORY: SRIVIDYA NATARAJAN

ART: APARAJITA NINAN

PRODUCTION: SANJIV PALLIWAL

Acknowledgements

SRIVIDYA NATARAJAN

My thanks to the readers of the draft version of "A Gardener" for insights, suggestions, encouragement: Joseph Mathai, Rhea John, Jerry Pinto, Sanjay Kak. (The shortcomings of the text, of course, are all my own.) And my thanks to Nigel and Richard for helping me find time to write.

APARAJITA NINAN

A massive thanks to Dad without whom the hands I drew would have looked like feet. S. Anand—a terror and a half—I blame all future grey hairs and great works on you. Srividya—for being my lighthouse—guiding me calmly from a distance. Alkazi Foundation, for letting me access their collection for research on costume and architecture. Mom, for unconditionally supporting this poor artist while other kids were on their way to millions...there is still hope! Finally, Anand, my unfailing source of love and support in cultivating this work and many more to come.

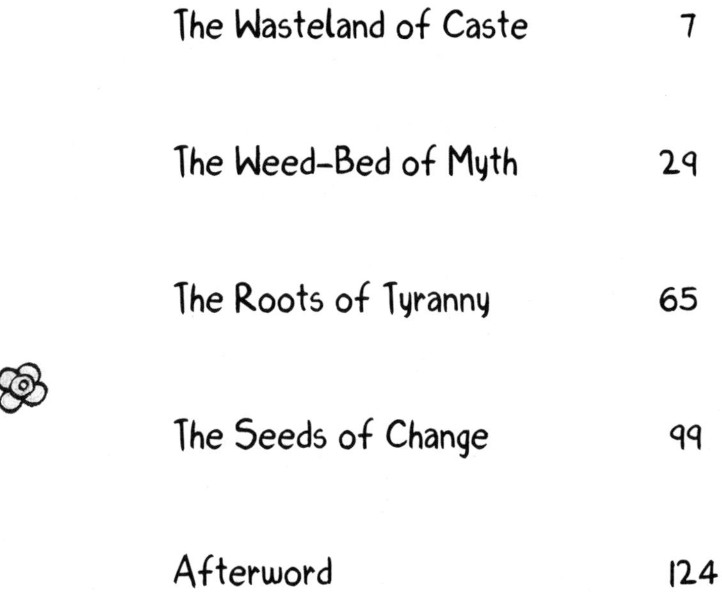

THE WASTELAND OF CASTE

NEW DELHI, 1 FEB 2010
TUITION

Vidya, I want to start doing the roughs for *Gulamgiri* this week. How far have you got with the script?

Patience, Appu. I've got the research done.

ISD
I've submitted the preface for my grad thesis, but I need to get the rest done before I leave Navayana. Can you hurry the script up a bit?

Son of a chamar whore—wrecking the property of your betters!
AAAAARGH!!
Sometimes I can understand why people want a superhero...
...in spandex and a cape, with unbelievable pecs...
...to swoop down out of the sky and kick the baddies to bits.

POONA, WESTERN INDIA, IN THE 1840s.
A HELLHOLE OF A TOWN. A MOB RUNS IT: A BRAHMAN MOB.
Pure wish-fulfilment. Would that change anything about oppression, Indian style?
How different are we now from how we were, say, in Jotiba Phule's time?
Pass the Gangajal, will you?
Caste is merely division of labour.
No, caste is systematic oppression.
HOWEVER, IT IS ESSENTIALLY A DVAIVARNIK SYSTEM...
THE PESHWAS, BRAHMANS INITIALLY APPOINTED BY SHIVAJI, AND SHARING POWER WITH HIS MARATHA SUCCESSORS, HAVE BROKEN AWAY TO CREATE THEIR OWN THEOCRACY, GOVERNED BY 'SCRIPTURAL' LAWS.

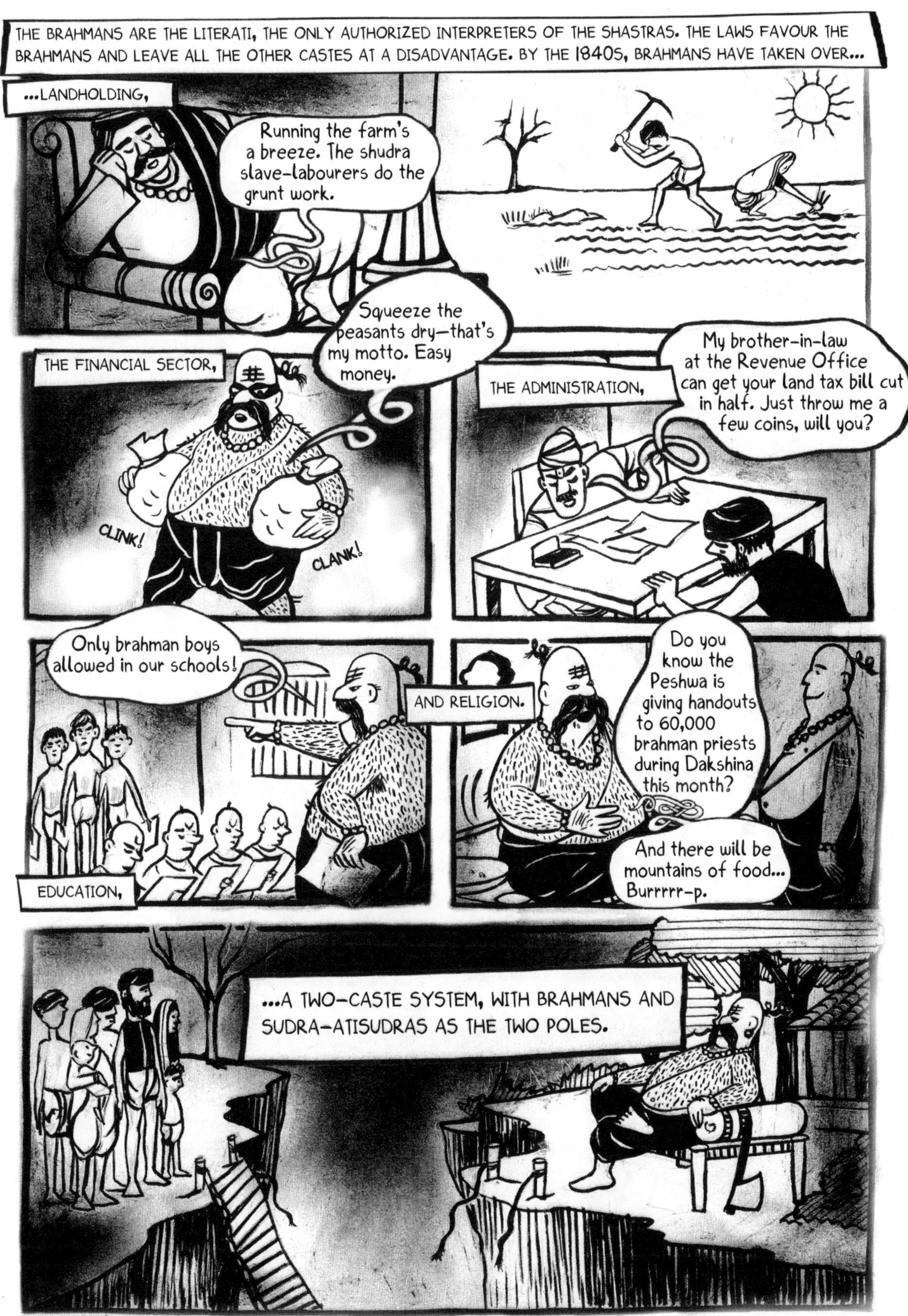
THE BRAHMANS ARE THE LITERATI, THE ONLY AUTHORIZED INTERPRETERS OF THE SHASTRAS. THE LAWS FAVOUR THE BRAHMANS AND LEAVE ALL THE OTHER CASTES AT A DISADVANTAGE. BY THE 1840S, BRAHMANS HAVE TAKEN OVER...
...LANDHOLDING,
Running the farm's a breeze. The shudra slave-labourers do the grunt work.
THE FINANCIAL SECTOR,
Squeeze the peasants dry—that's my motto. Easy money.
CLINK!
CLANK!
THE ADMINISTRATION,
My brother-in-law at the Revenue Office can get your land tax bill cut in half. Just throw me a few coins, will you?
EDUCATION,
Only brahman boys allowed in our schools!
AND RELIGION.
Do you know the Peshwa is giving handouts to 60,000 brahman priests during Dakshina this month?
And there will be mountains of food... Burrrrr-p.
...A TWO-CASTE SYSTEM, WITH BRAHMANS AND SUDRA-ATISUDRAS AS THE TWO POLES.

3 FEB 2010
WATCH IT!
VROOOM!
SCREEECH!
PAARP!
Hi Vidya, Looking over your notes on Savitribai Phule. I'm on my way to my internship, dodging Delhi traffic...
I'm seeing Savitribai in my head...
POONA, 1848
A YOUNG WOMAN—A GIRL, SHE'S SEVENTEEN—IS ON HER WAY TO WORK, DODGING MISSILES.
SPLAT!
SPLASH!
SPIT!
Shameless sudra slut!
So you think you can *teach school* like a *man*?
SNAKEWOMAN!
Go back to the kitchen where you belong!

WANTED
Savitri Phule, for educating sudra and atisudra girls
BANG! BANG!
EDUCATION HAS ALWAYS BEEN MORE ELUSIVE FOR SOME PEOPLE THAN FOR OTHERS.
Nigger!
Ape!
1957. LITTLE ROCK, ARKANSAS—AFRICAN AMERICAN STUDENTS WERE DENIED ENTRANCE TO THE SCHOOL.
HERE IN POONA, NONE OF THE BRAHMAN BIGWIGS WANTS SAVITRIBAI'S 'LOW CASTE' CHARGES TO GET AN EDUCATION.
I wonder how much longer I can stand this... and how much longer we will live in this town.

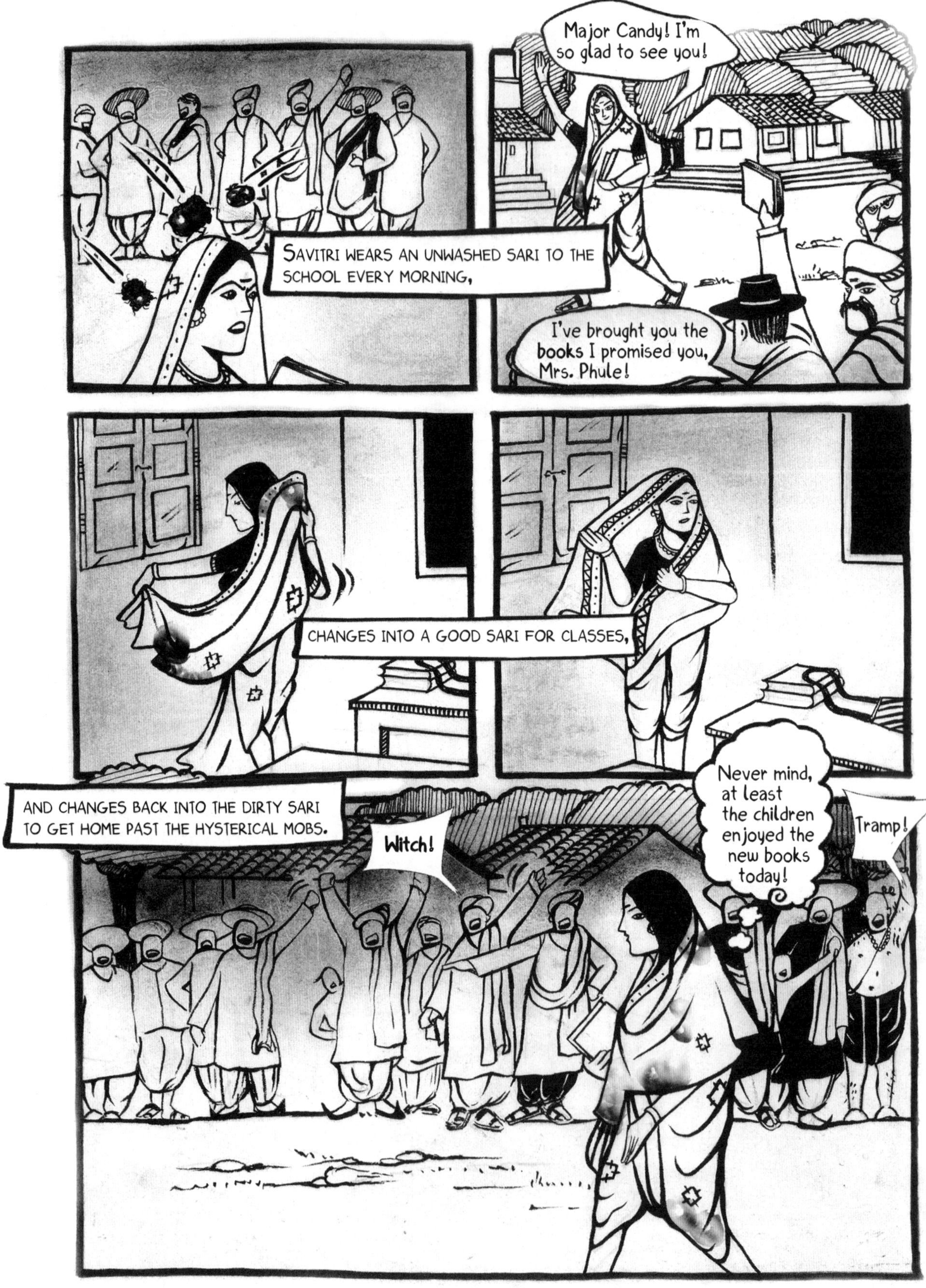
Savitri wears an unwashed sari to the school every morning,
Major Candy! I'm so glad to see you!
I've brought you the books I promised you, Mrs. Phule!
Changes into a good sari for classes,
And changes back into the dirty sari to get home past the hysterical mobs.
Witch!
Never mind, at least the children enjoyed the new books today!
Tramp!

THAT NIGHT...
Govindrao, how dare your son admit these sudra children to his school!
And untouchable children! And girls!
What do girls want with school?
We shouldn't have kept quiet when you—a lowly mali—educated your boy!
We even accepted Jotirao educating his wife. But letting her go out to teach!
Like some public woman! Unheard of!
Against our religion! Can't you control your daughter-in-law?
If you don't stop your son and daughter-in-law, Govindrao, blood will be shed.
Joti, Savitri, my children. This is the final straw—our lives are being threatened. Either give up the school or stop living under my roof.
This is my life's work, father.

My friends did say that educating you would prove a bad idea. It has given you ideas above your station.
Is that why you took me out of school?
We are cultivators of the earth. I should never have let you go back to school. Joti, I cannot permit this work to continue.
Then, much as I love and respect you, we will have to part ways. I'm sorry.
THE COUPLE MOVED OUT OF GOVINDRAO'S HOUSE.
Good riddance.
SAVITRI NEVER GAVE UP, EVEN THOUGH JOTIRAO AND SHE FACED THE SAME PROBLEMS WHEREVER THEY WENT.
There are many idiots here, as in Poona, who poison people's minds and spread canards against us. But why should we fear them and abandon this noble cause we have undertaken?...The future belongs to us.

4 FEB 2010
Savitribai is amazing! A woman ahead of her times. I can identify with her. Married at eight. Hungry for an education and eager to change her world.
As a child, I read about Lakshmibai, I read about Sarojini Naidu...
I never read about Savitribai Phule. We honour teachers on Radhakrishnan's birthday, not on hers. I guess she has been erased, like other nonbrahman role models, from history.
When Jotiba began writing *Gulamgiri*, Savitribai had worked at his side and shared his vision for some thirty years.
She headed the women's wing of the Truthseekers' Society, which promoted equality among human beings and rational thought, and rejected brahmanical ritual.
NONBRAHMAN FEMALE ACTIVIST AND THINKER. WIFE OF BAD PERSON WHO CHALLENGED THE HINDU WAY OF LIFE. **CENSORED.**

We need a blueprint for change,
for human equality,
JOTIBA READS FROM THOMAS PAINE, *RIGHTS OF MAN*
"When despotism has established itself for ages in a country...
the original hereditary despotism, resident in the person the king, divides and sub-divides itsel into a thousand shapes and forms..."
He could be talking of brahmanical Hinduism.

for a society in which all human beings enjoy the same rights.
Naturally, Jotiba isn't looking for this blueprint in the Hindu shastras.
Please allow me to quote from the French National Assembly's Declaration of Rights...
"Men are born, and always continue, free and equal in respect of their rights...
The end of all political associations is the preservation of the natural and imprescriptible rights of man...
these rights are
liberty,
property,
security,
and resistance of oppression."

LIBERTY
FRATERNITY
The future belongs to us!
Without education wisdom was lost!
Be your own light!
He who invented god is a fool!
Pandit, you've got it wrong!
Workers of the world, unite!
Let a hundred flowers bloom!
There is no such thing as part freedom.
Slavery, a haven for the death penalty.
Revolution is not a bed of roses.
Peace! Land! Bread!
Educate! Organise! Agitate!
Hasta la Victoria Siempre!
I have a dream...
I am hungry for justice!
What do we want? Azadi!

EQUALITY
By any means necessary!
End the rule of the queen!
Inquilab Zindabad!

God gave freedom to all people,
including the sudras and atisudras, to enjoy all the things he created in this world.
The brahmans confiscated the rights of all others and became all-powerful.
FIZZZZZZLE
Europeans and Americans, to their great shame, did the same thing to the people they enslaved.
They treated people as beasts of burden,
harnessing them to ploughs like bullocks,
whipping them,
starving them,
cruelly estranging them from their families.

But several generous people fought against slavery, and in the end, the Americans freed their slaves from the clutches of their tormentors...
I have plowed and reaped and husked and chopped and mowed, and can any man do more than that?
SOJOURNER TRUTH
I was the conductor of the Underground Railroad for eight years, and I can say... I never ran my train off the track and I never lost a passenger...
Lord, keep us safe one more day from the traps of the slave-catchers—tomorrow we will be in Canada, land of freedom.
ST CATHARINE'S 40 MILES
$100 REWARD RAN AWAY FROM RICHMOND 2 JUNE, WM. N. HARRIS, NEGRO MAN BELONGING TO MR. EZRA WAYNE OF HANOVER COUNTY. 26 YEARS, RUGGED BUILD, QUITE BLACK, NO FRONT TEETH.'
HARRIET TUBMAN
The sudras and atisudras will appreciate the importance of this history of emancipation—they know what slavery is like...

...going back to the days of Manu, the brahman Lawmaker.
अग्निमीळे
पुरोहितं
यज्ञस्य
देवमृत्विजम्
'If the sudra intentionally listens to the Veda with the intention of committing it to memory, his ears should be filled with molten lead; if he utters the veda, then his tongue should be cut off; if he has mastered the veda his body should be cut to pieces.' Verse 4, Ch XII
MANUSMRITI 2nd CENTURY C.E.
MANUSMRITI
2nd CENTURY C.E.

The **strange fruit** that Abel Meeropol saw, and Billie Holiday sang in 1939...
Southern trees bear strange fruit,
Blood on the leaves and blood at the root,
Black body swinging in the Southern breeze,
Strange fruit hanging from the poplar trees.
Pastoral scene of the gallant South,
The bulging eyes and the twisted mouth,
Scent of magnolia sweet and fresh,
Then the sudden smell of burning flesh!
Here is fruit for the crows to pluck,
For the rain to gather, for the wind to suck,
For the sun to rot, for the tree to drop,
Here is a strange and bitter crop.

DAILY NEWS AND A

LORE, SUNDAY, APRIL 25, 2010

DALIT CHILDREN AMONG 15 RESCUE FROM BONDAGE IN TAMIL NADU

Nivedita Singh TAMIL NADU

Nine Dalit children were among 15 persons rescued from bondage by revenue officials from a brick kiln near Erode in Tamil Nadu, district officials said. Benjamin Prabhu, revenue divisional officer, Erode said officials had acted on information that 15 persons of Kattuserry village in Nagapattinam district were being forced to work as bonded labourers in a brick kiln at Kalingarayanpalayam, 12km from Erode.The officials went to the kiln yesterday and spoke to the 15 persons, belonging to three families. One of them alleged that they were not being paid proper wages and that their children are suffering for want of education.The officials registered cases under SC/ST (Prevention of Atrocities) Act, Minimum Wages Act and abolition of bonded labour act against the kiln owner.The rescued were sent back to their native town after being given a part of Rs10,000 to be granted as per government rules. The balance would be given later after receiving funds, they said. One of the bonded labourers reportedly received Rs30,000 as advance from the owner and another, Rs20,000. The owner said the amounts were adjusted against their wages. He also claimed that he had not violated any rules and that all the families were given proper wages.

SLAVERY OPPRESSION
To struggle against slavery, to liberate the slaves from the tyranny of oppression—a free man could face danger and risk his life for this noble purpose...
So could a free woman!
Jotiba and Savitribai were fierce gardeners in the wasteland of caste. To build a garden, you must first dig up the weeds.

THE WEED-BED OF MYTH

8 MARCH 2010
HINDU MYTHOLOGY
Oh look, good old Amar Chitra Katha comics.
They have a TV series now.
I read them in class, hidden inside my Chemistry textbook... remember how the women were always impossibly curvy?
And the good guys were always fair and the baddies, the rakshasas, were always dung-green?
Hindu mythology has a lot to answer for, no? You know, Phule was one of the few people who asked the question: so **who** made up these stories? **Who** derived legitimacy from these legends?
MAHABHARAT
Look at this one— Yudishthira is saying, 'Every varna should adhere to its own dharma.'

Ahh... two.
Dhondiba, how many spoons of sugar?
Several European scholars said the Aryans came to India from outside. Most brahman scholars agreed with them, because that made them kin to Europeans. So **who** were the rightful inheritors of this land and **who** were the interlopers?
Listen to Jotiba argue his case with his friend Dhondiba.

The brahmans were created from the mouth of Brahma.

So far, so good.

Thank god someone invented the sanitary pad!

Now tell me, is there any written evidence that Brahma's mouth, which gave birth to the brahmans, menstruated every month, and that he had to sit in seclusion for four days?

Since Brahma had vaginas in four places—mouth, arms, groin and legs (since the four varnas were born out of these four parts) each of them must have menstruated for at least four days each, and he must have sat in seclusion, as an unclean person, for sixteen days each month. Then who did the chores?
And one wonders why Seshasayee, who had a wife, Lakshmi, had to be the one who gave birth to Brahma. Does it say anywhere if Brahma had eight breasts, four belly-buttons, four sets of genitals and four anuses?
This story is just full of holes. The truth is...

the Aryans, who call themselves brahmans today are said to be descendents of the Indo-European race—the same stock as Persians, Medes and other Iranians.
They crossed the great Himalayan divide to the Hindu Kush where they were confronted by the aborigines.
What followed was a struggle for ascendancy, about which the brahmans have fabricated absurd myths in their Vedas and passed them off as history.

THE WARS OF THE DEVAS AND DAITYAS OR THE RAKSHASAS, ABOUT WHICH SO MANY FICTIONS ARE FOUND SCATTERED THROUGH THE SACRED BOOKS OF THE BRAHMANS, ARE CERTAINLY A REFERENCE TO THIS PRIMEVAL STRUGGLE.

So how did the first Aryans get here?
They came by sea.
In ships?
In fast-moving canoes.
That was why the chief of the earliest horde was called Matsya.

But the Brahmans have written that Matsya was born of a fish.

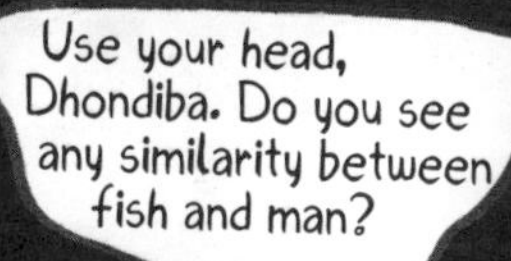
Use your head, Dhondiba. Do you see any similarity between fish and man?

If this chief was born of a fish who laid her eggs in the water, how did the human baby survive in the water?
If the fish mother brought it to land, how did she swim out of the water?
Fishy, don't you think, the brahman story of Vishnu's first avatar?
Distinctly. What happened next?

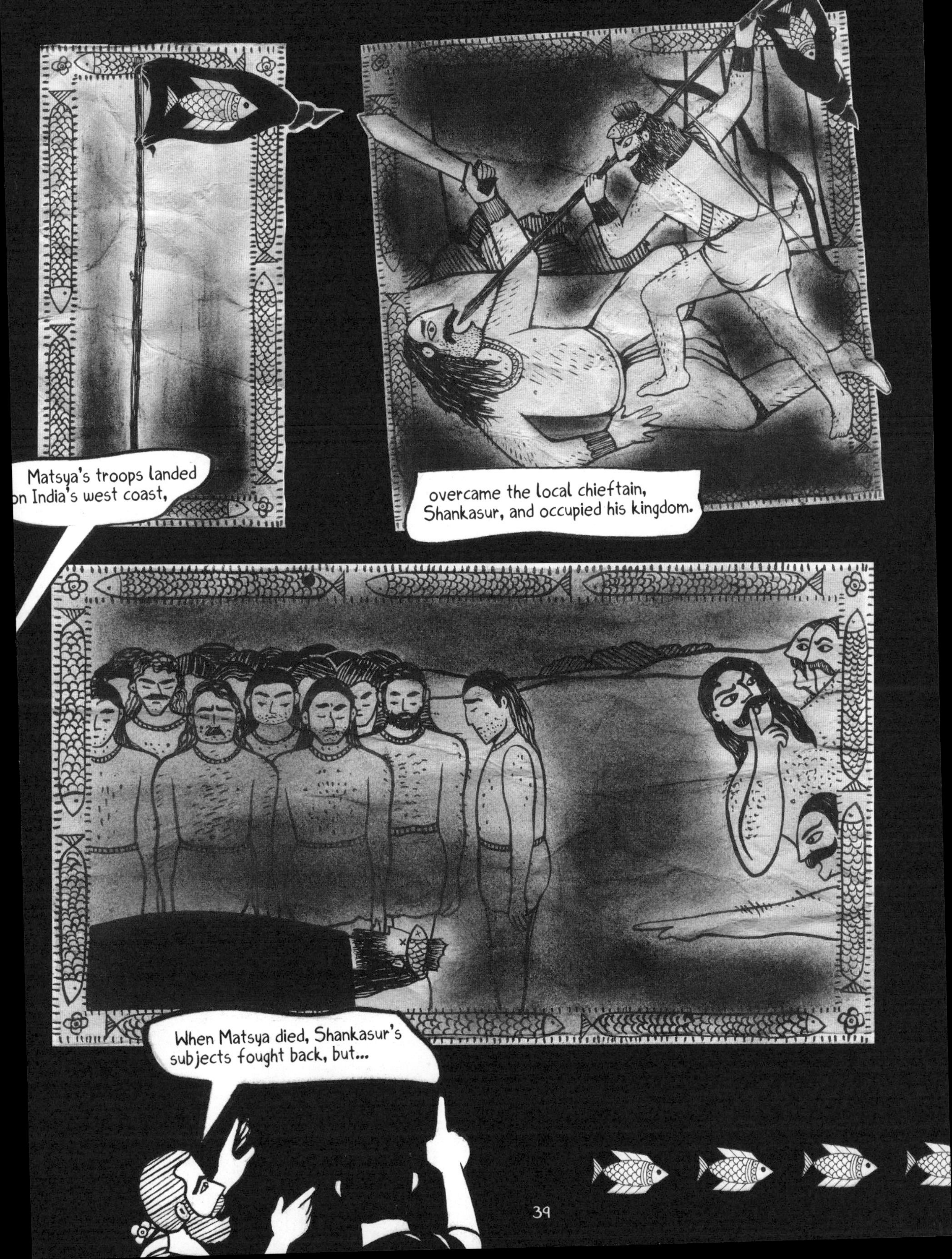

Matsya's troops landed
on India's west coast,

overcame the local chieftain,
Shankasur, and occupied his kingdom.

When Matsya died, Shankasur's
subjects fought back, but...

another wave of invaders from Iran came to the rescue of their predecessors,
in boats that travelled slowly like tortoises...

The indigenous people were harried by Kachcha's troops and had to flee to the mountains.
After Kachcha died, Varaha became chief of the Aryan hordes...
Hence the tale of the second avatar of Vishnu, Kachha the tortoise...
?
I won't even ask if Kachcha was born of a tortoise.

The third incarnation, born of a boar, says the Bhagawata...

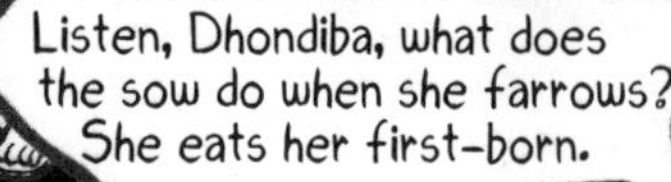

So the all-seeing Vishnu, in the form of Varaha, must have known his older sibling had been eaten.

God's own mother committing infanticide and God not preventing it!

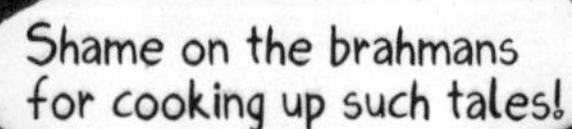

Varaha probably got his name from the destruction he wrought.
And shame on the rest of us for setting these brahmans up as holy!

Then Narsimha took over—
a greedy, scheming, brutal man.

To seize the local chief Hiranyakashyapu's kingdom, he worked on the mind of his young son Prahlad, who betrayed his father.

Narsimha wore a lion's mask, crept into the palace at night...

leapt
...hid behind a pillar until Hiranyakashyapu was asleep,

on
him,

and tore his belly open.

The actions of a coward. So much for the Narsimha avatar.

The brahmans used their myths like false letters of introduction to impose on the credulity of the other castes.
The brahmans had oppressed these castes so much and reduced them to such a state of ignorance that when they cunningly showed them the books and told them they were written by God himself...
...the other castes fell victim to their trickery.

Observe how the other castes accept the brahman perspective on the exploits of kshatriya heroes like **Bali.**
A brave soldier, a descendant of Prahlad, Bali rescued several small chieftains from the harassment of trouble-mongers and brought them under his rule.
Then he started expanding the frontiers of his kingdom.

What a great king Bali was! How his subjects prospered during his reign!
This is why on Dasara day, kshatriya women wave earthen lamps before their husbands' faces and wish for the kingdom of Bali to come again.
During Bali's reign, **Vamana** was the chief leader of the enemies, the brahmans. He collected an army to quell Bali.
They fought
for
eight days.
On the
...and Vamana looted Bali's capital.

eighth day
of battle,
Bali was
...killed,
I love how Phule shows you that myths are interpreted differently by different communities. In my native Kerala, folk songs praise the casteless kingdom of the just king, Maveli (Mahabali), and he is still honoured every year during the Onam harvest festival. Brahman narratives claim that Onam marks the birth of the dwarf-priest Vamana.

Give me three feet of land as my dakshina.

Certainly.
ONE
VAMANA'S FOOT COVERS FIRST THE EARTH...THEN

But the brahman myth gives us the improbable story of Vamana crushing Bali underfoot.

TWO
THE SKY, AND THEN...

Where shall I put my third step?
THREE
I offer my head.
BALI'S HEAD.

Consider this:
SQUISH
If the monster Vamana covered the whole earth with his first step, how many villages must have been crushed under his foot!
If he had put his second step in the sky, how many stars must have collided with each other and been ground to dust!

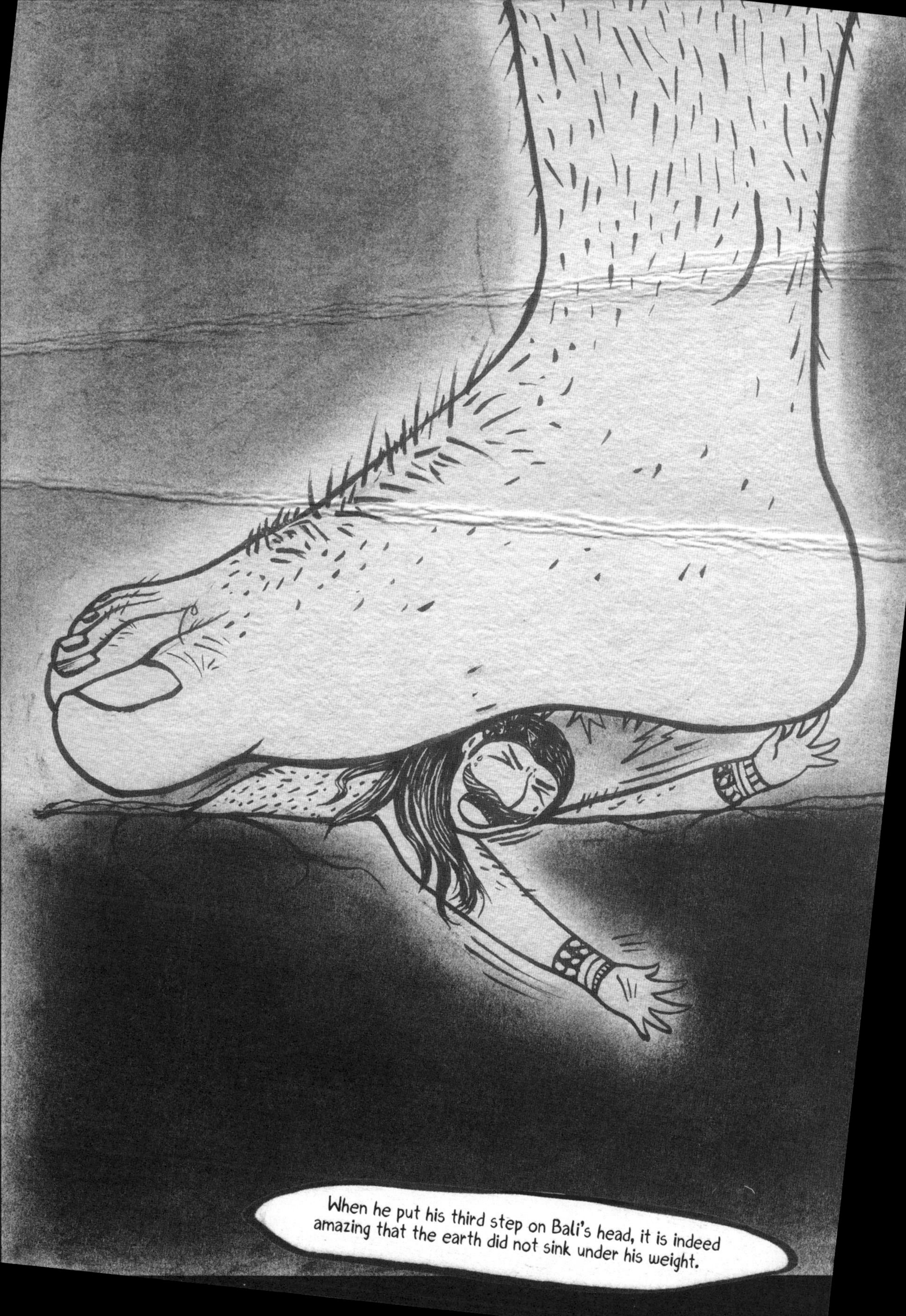
When he put his third step on Bali's head, it is indeed amazing that the earth did not sink under his weight.

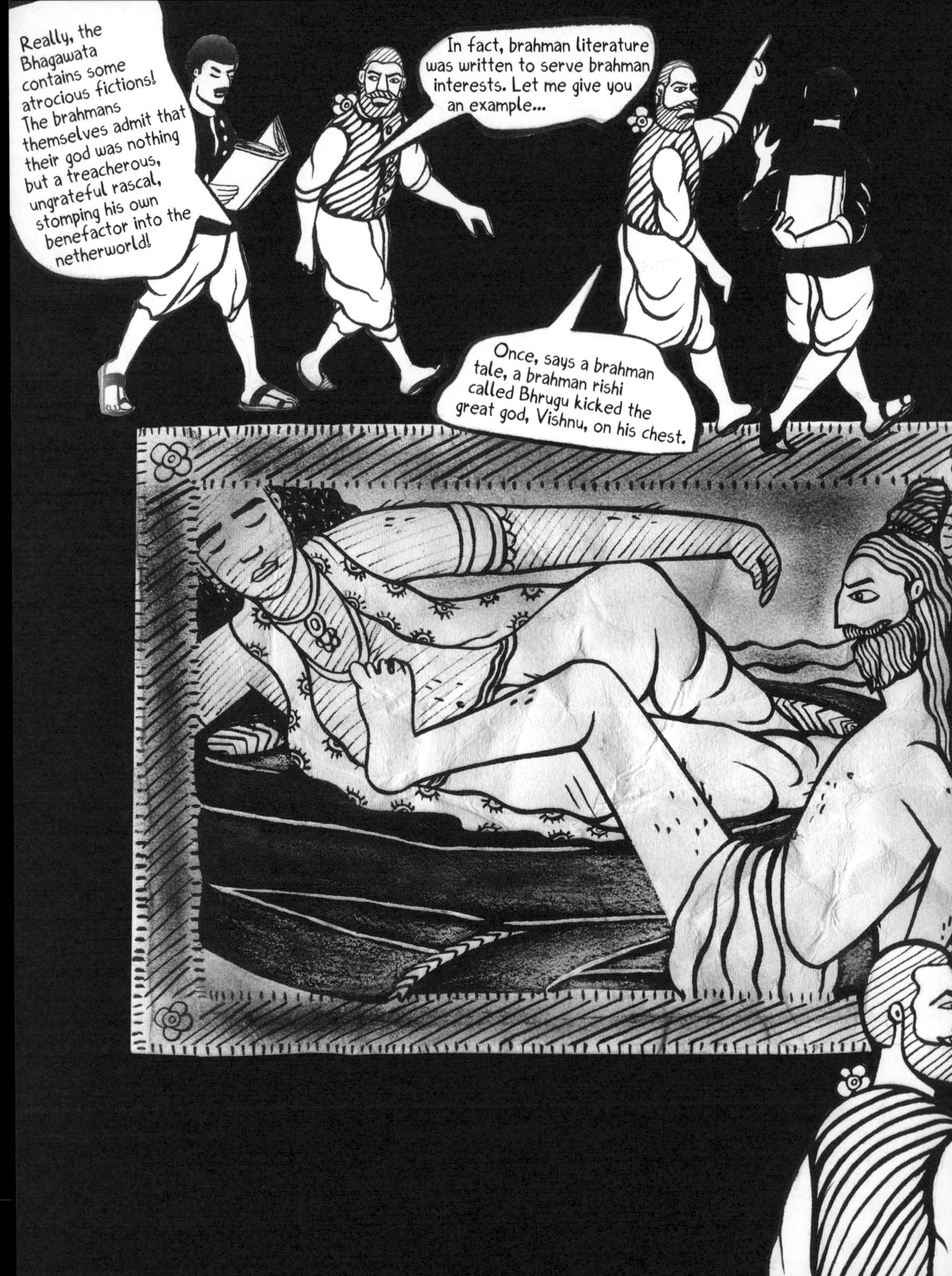
Really, the Bhagawata contains some atrocious fictions! The brahmans themselves admit that their god was nothing but a treacherous, ungrateful rascal, stomping his own benefactor into the netherworld!
In fact, brahman literature was written to serve brahman interests. Let me give you an example...
Once, says a brahman tale, a brahman rishi called Bhrugu kicked the great god, Vishnu, on his chest.

Now, instead of getting angry, the god began to massage the offending foot, arguing that the kick must have hurt it.
A cleverly constructed yarn. The moral?
When Lord Vishnu himself could suffer a kick so patiently, why should the sudras complain about the kicks, blows and murderous assaults of the brahmans?

On to the next avatar: Parashuram. He lived by such a barbarous code,

that he did not hesitate to behead his own mother, Renuka.

he captured pregnant kshatriya women, imprisoned them...

He hunted down all the male progeny of the kshatriya clans,
and killed their male children as they were born.

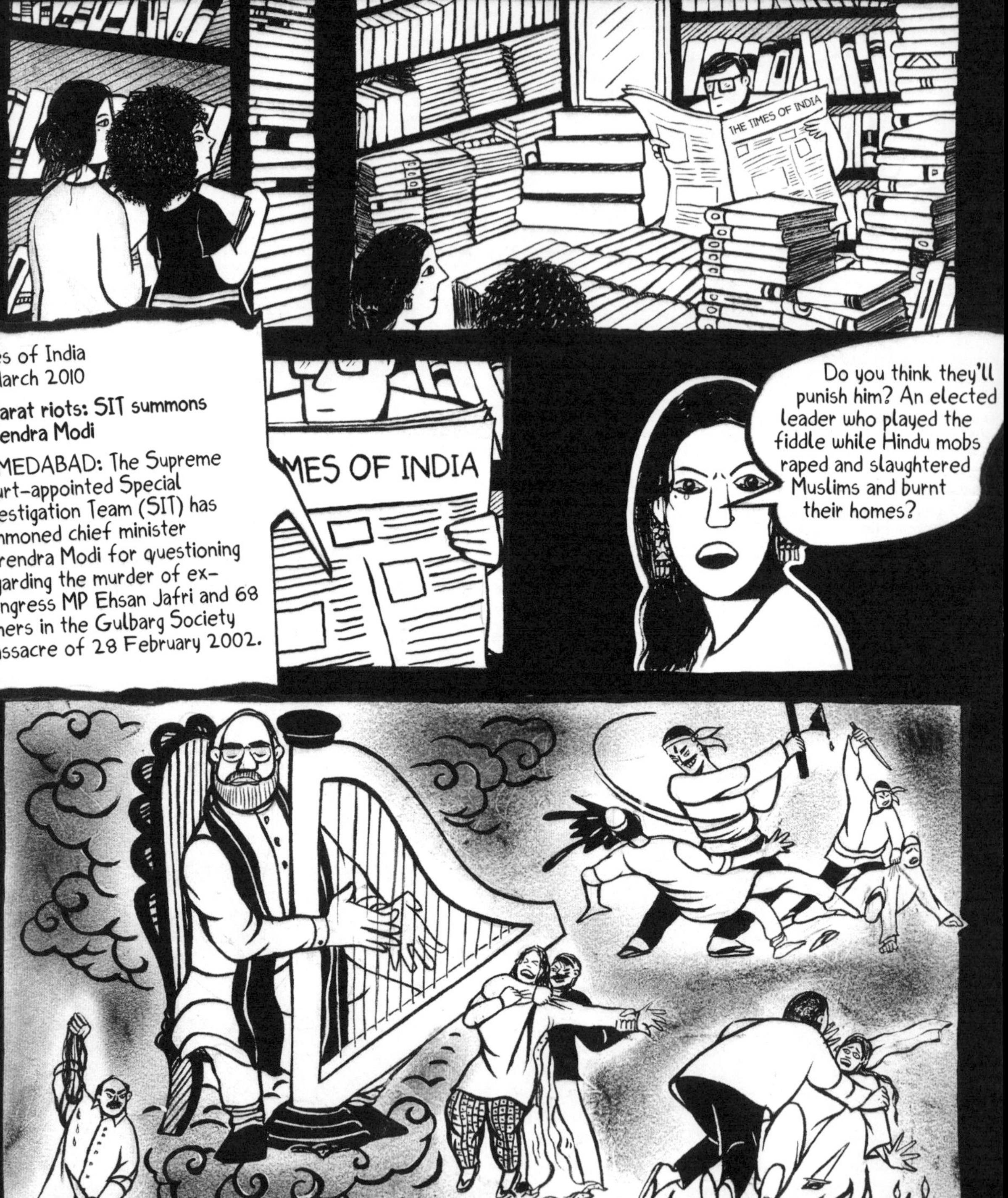

Times of India
12 March 2010

Gujarat riots: SIT summons Narendra Modi

AHMEDABAD: The Supreme Court-appointed Special Investigation Team (SIT) has summoned chief minister Narendra Modi for questioning regarding the murder of ex-Congress MP Ehsan Jafri and 68 others in the Gulbarg Society massacre of 28 February 2002.

Some Hindu fanatics boasted of having ripped foetuses from Muslim women's wombs.
Parashuram, updated for the 21st century, Hindutva-style. I love how deliberately outrageous Phule is when he walks the borderland between mythology and history. He reminds one that history is story too.

THE ROOTS OF TYRANNY

MIDLANDS
BOOK
SHOP
History, like myth, changes depending on who writes it, who reads it. 
Jotiba makes you shift your perspective on the Aryans, for instance...

PHULE'S PERSPECTIVE

BRAHMAN'S PERSPECTIVE

ARYANS

INVADERS

USURPERS

KILLERS OF ABORIGINAL DASYUS

INDO-EUROPEANS

TRUE INDIANS

RAKSHASAS

INDIGENOUS PEOPLE WITH A FAR GREATER RIGHT TO CLAIM OWNERSHIP OF INDIA

DARK-SKINNED MONSTERS

DEMONS

DESECRATORS OF BRAHMAN RITES AND SACRIFICES

PHULE'S PERSPECTIVE

BRAHMAN'S PERSPECTIVE

MATSYA

SYMBOL OF FOREIGN (ARYAN) INVASION BY SEA

AVATAR OF GOD VISHNU

VAMANA

RIGHTEOUS RESTORER OF THE RULE OF BRAHMANS

DECEIVER

SLIMEBAG

DESTROYER OF THE GOLDEN AGE OF BALI

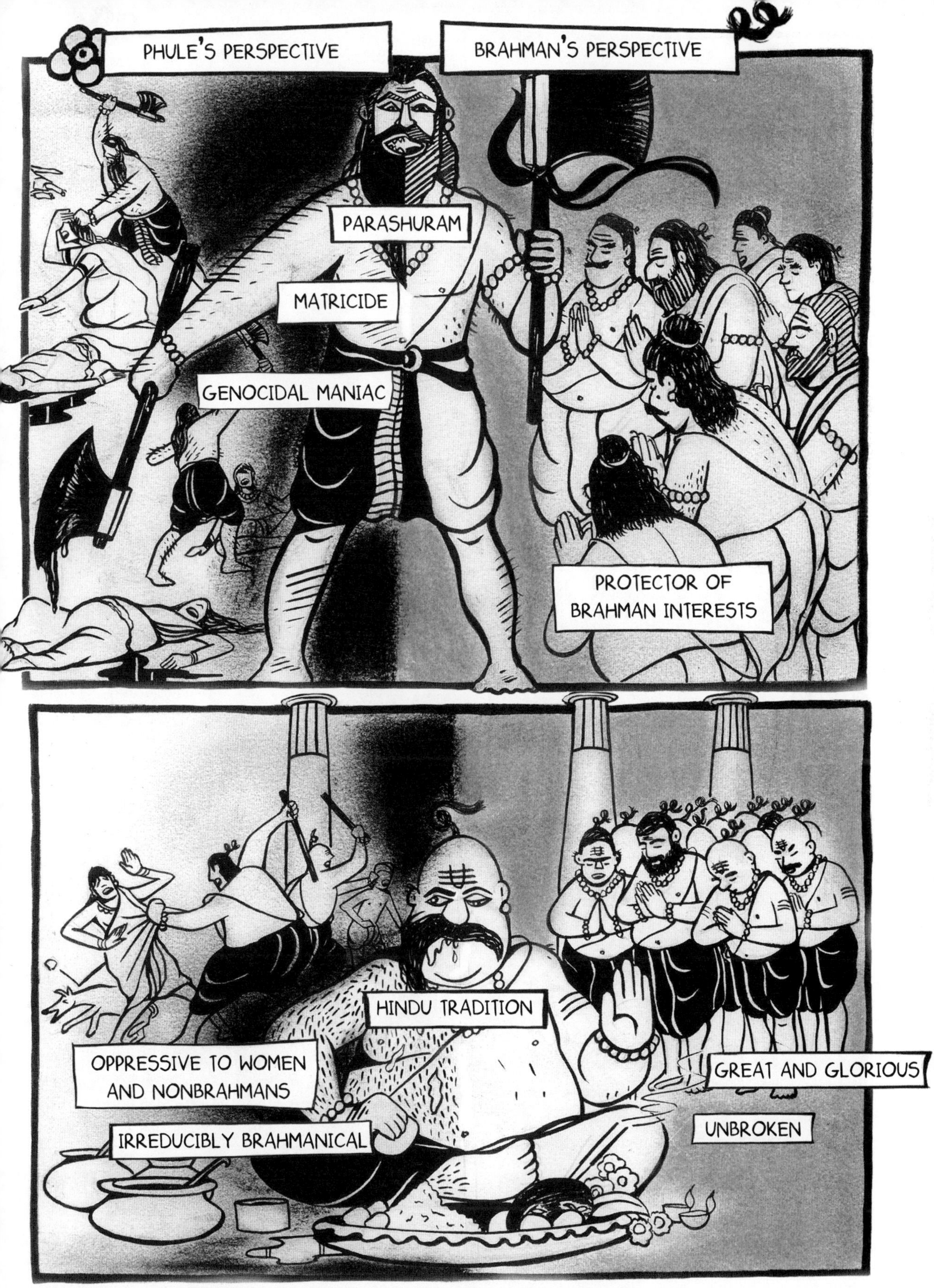
PHULE'S PERSPECTIVE
BRAHMAN'S PERSPECTIVE
PARASHURAM
MATRICIDE
GENOCIDAL MANIAC
PROTECTOR OF BRAHMAN INTERESTS
HINDU TRADITION
OPPRESSIVE TO WOMEN AND NONBRAHMANS
IRREDUCIBLY BRAHMANICAL
GREAT AND GLORIOUS
UNBROKEN

We believe that Phule is a true patriot, upholding the rights of all Indians.
While the nationalists believe that he is a comprador admirer of European liberalism and not a patriot.

We are the Bhudevas: the lords of this earth.
The Aryans who came to India appear to have been a race imbued with very high notions of self; they were extremely cunning, arrogant and bigoted.
They settled on the banks of the Ganges,
and then gradually spread over the whole of India...
HINDU KUSH MOUNTAINS
RIVER INDUS
RIVER YAMUNA
RIVER GANGA
ARABIAN SEA
RIVER NARMADA

MANUSMRITI
...carrying with them their absurd mythology, their caste hierarchy,
and the code of inhuman laws that allowed them to keep a hold on all the people they encountered.

IN ORDER TO KEEP A BETTER HOLD ON THE PEOPLE THEY DEVISED THAT WEIRD SYSTEM OF MYTHOLOGY, THE ORDINATION OF CASTE, AND THE CODE OF CRUEL AND INHUMAN LAWS TO WHICH WE CAN FIND NO PARALLEL AMONGST OTHER NATIONS.

THE HIGHEST RIGHTS, THE HIGHEST PRIVILEGES AND GIFTS, AND EVERYTHING THAT WOULD MAKE THE LIFE OF A BRAHMAN EASY, SMOOTH AND HAPPY—EVERYTHING THAT WOULD CONSERVE OR FLATTER THEIR SELF-PRIDE—WERE SPECIALLY INCULCATED AND ENJOINED, WHEREAS THE SUDRAS AND ATISUDRAS WERE REGARDED WITH SUPREME HATRED AND CONTEMPT AND THE COMMONEST RIGHTS OF HUMANITY WERE DENIED THEM. THEIR TOUCH, NAY EVEN THEIR SHADOW, IS DEEMED A POLLUTION.

After Brahma's death the brahmans collected his writings as the three Vedas. They added several stories and myths and created a fourth Veda.
Later the brahmans compiled all their magical incantations and their silly tales, and composed several new books, like the smritis, shastras, puranas, samhitas, out of them.

A BRAHMIN IS ...

HE IS THE LORD OF THE UNIVERSE.

HE IS EQUAL TO GOD HIMSELF.

HE IS TO BE WORSHIPPED, SERVED AND RESPECTED BY ALL.

HE CANNOT BE SLAIN, NOT EVEN BY A KING.

HE CANNOT GIVE ANY ADVICE TO A SUDRA.

HE CAN COHABIT EVEN WITH A SUDRA'S LAWFUL WIFE.

HE CANNOT BE TAXED.

Many of the laws in the *Manusmriti* had to do with the mandatory subservience of the sudras. For instance..
'A brahman may compel a man of the servile class to perform servile duty because such a man was created by the Almighty only for the purpose of serving brahmans.'
'A sudra, though emancipated by his master, is not released from a state of servitude. For, being born in a state natural to him, by whom can he be divested of his attributes?'
To enslave the minds of the people they conquered, the brahmans attributed the most immoral, inhuman, unjust actions and deeds to that Being who is our Creator. Thus did the brahmans convince the poor ignorant people that their slavery was justified even in the eyes of god.

Having conquered much of India,
and having created laws to suit themselves,
the Aryans abandoned their warmongering and created a great rigmarole of their purity and religiosity.
Look at this news item...
Figures, huh, when you think about what Phule was saying about the holier-than-thou brahman attitude?
Deccan Herald
20 March 2010
Karnataka bans cow slaughter
BENGALURU: The Karnataka Assembly passed the Prevention of Slaughter and Preservation of Cattle Bill, 2010 on Friday, 19 March, making cow slaughter a punishable and a nonbailable offense.
I ♡ BEEF
So if you kill a cow, you can go to prison for one to seven years and pay a fine of Rs 25,000! The Indian nation is still a Hindu nation, the 'Indian diet' a brahmanical diet.

To this day the brahmans deceive the gullible kunbis and malis with their yapping—their incantations and rituals—and fatten themselves on the offerings of the poor and the hardworking.
You're going to need a big sacrifice to save your mother's life—it will cost you Rs 250.
If you want your daughter to be married with the proper rituals, you'd better pay up.
The brahmans strictly prohibited the education of the sudras so as to keep them ignorant. This gave the brahmans the authority to make whatever changes they wanted in the so-called sacred books.
SANATAN DHARAM SCHOOL (SUDRAS NOT ALLOWED)
These changes kept pace with their own selfish interests.
Take your kids out of the school!
If you don't, we will burn your huts and your crops!

Later on, one great champion of the downtrodden, the sage and lover of the truth, Baliraja, preached that god had given us the true and holy knowledge and had granted everyone an equal right to it.
Millions became followers of this Baliraja in Europe, including the ancestors of great thinkers like Thomas Paine.

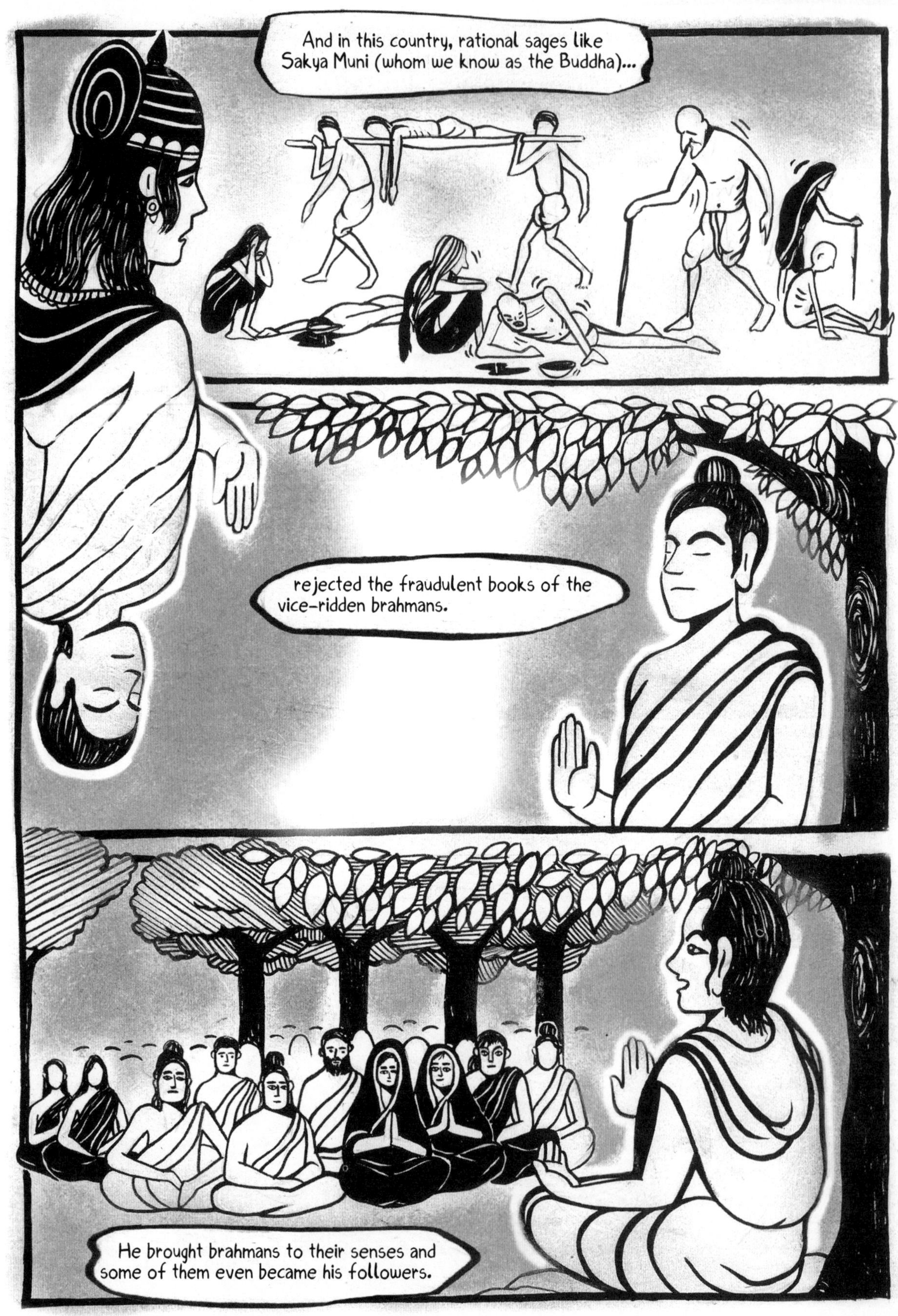
And in this country, rational sages like Sakya Muni (whom we know as the Buddha)...
rejected the fraudulent books of the vice-ridden brahmans.
He brought brahmans to their senses and some of them even became his followers.

But the devious brahman scholar
Adi Sankara used his twisted intellect
to re-establish brahman domination
in the 12th century.
His followers killed
several Buddhists by crushing
them in oil presses...
and burnt the most
precious Buddhist books,
except the Amarkosha.

Still later, towards the end of the rule of the infamous brahman king Baji Rao, several American and Scottish missionaries, followers of the Baliraja in the West, preached to the sudras and freed them from the rope of brahman slavery.
So the wily brahmans began trying to drive the British government out of this country before the friendship between the missionaries and the sudras matured further.
Don't listen to these low-caste interlopers! We Hindus—we brahmans, in fact—are the only true Indians!

A man who attacks the Hindu faith is a traitor to his country!

There's something I learnt about Jotiba some years after we were married.

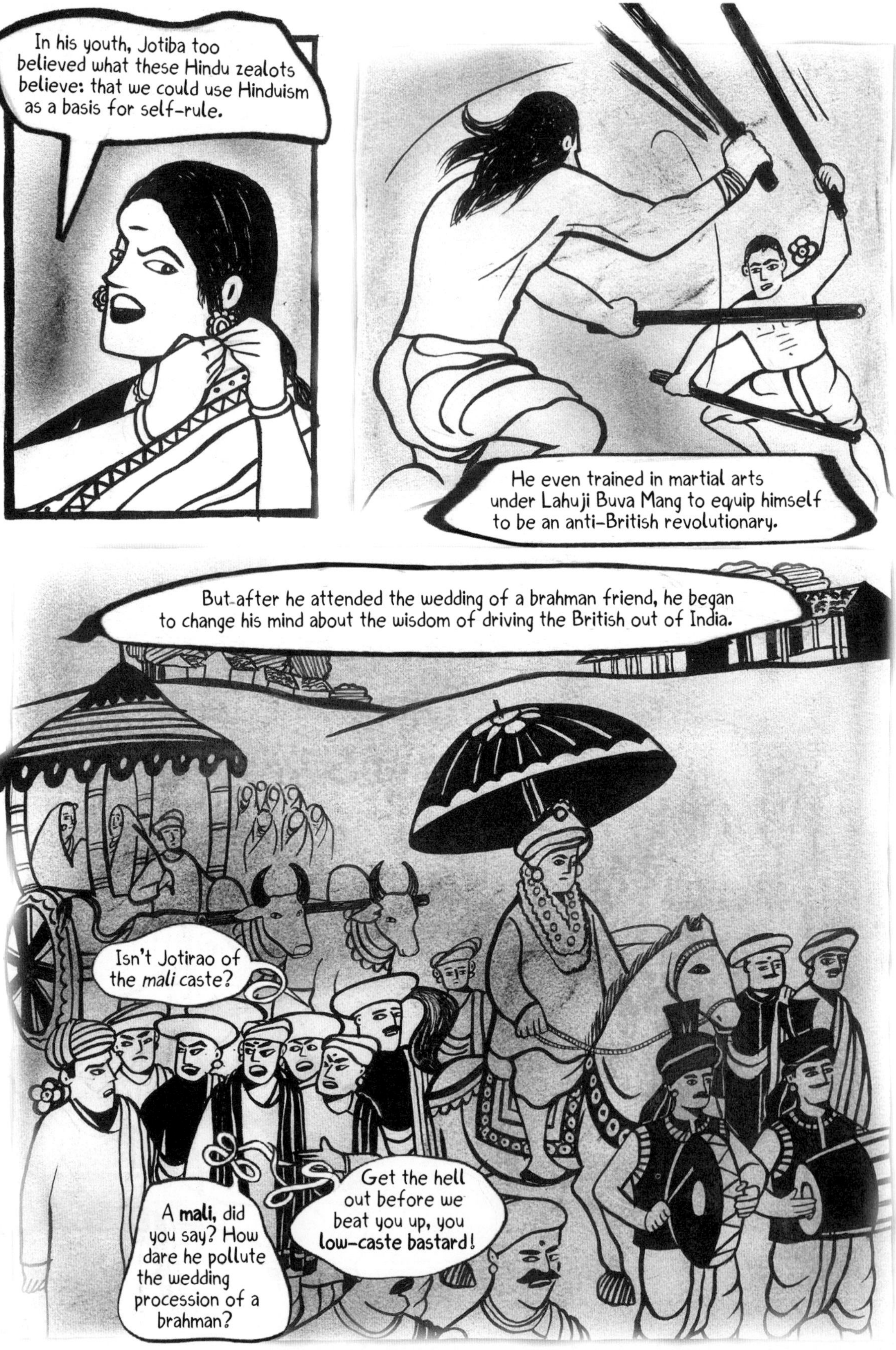

But after he attended the wedding of a brahman friend, he began to change his mind about the wisdom of driving the British out of India.

Isn't Jotirao of the *mali* caste?

A **mali,** did you say? How dare he pollute the wedding procession of a brahman?

Get the hell out before we beat you up, you **low-caste bastard!**

What allowed them to humiliate me like that?
In Hindu society, Joti, each of us must accept his lot.
It is not our job to fight against caste.
That is too dangerous.
So in a situation in which patriots and nationalists proudly proclaim themselves Hindus, Jotiba is the odd man out.

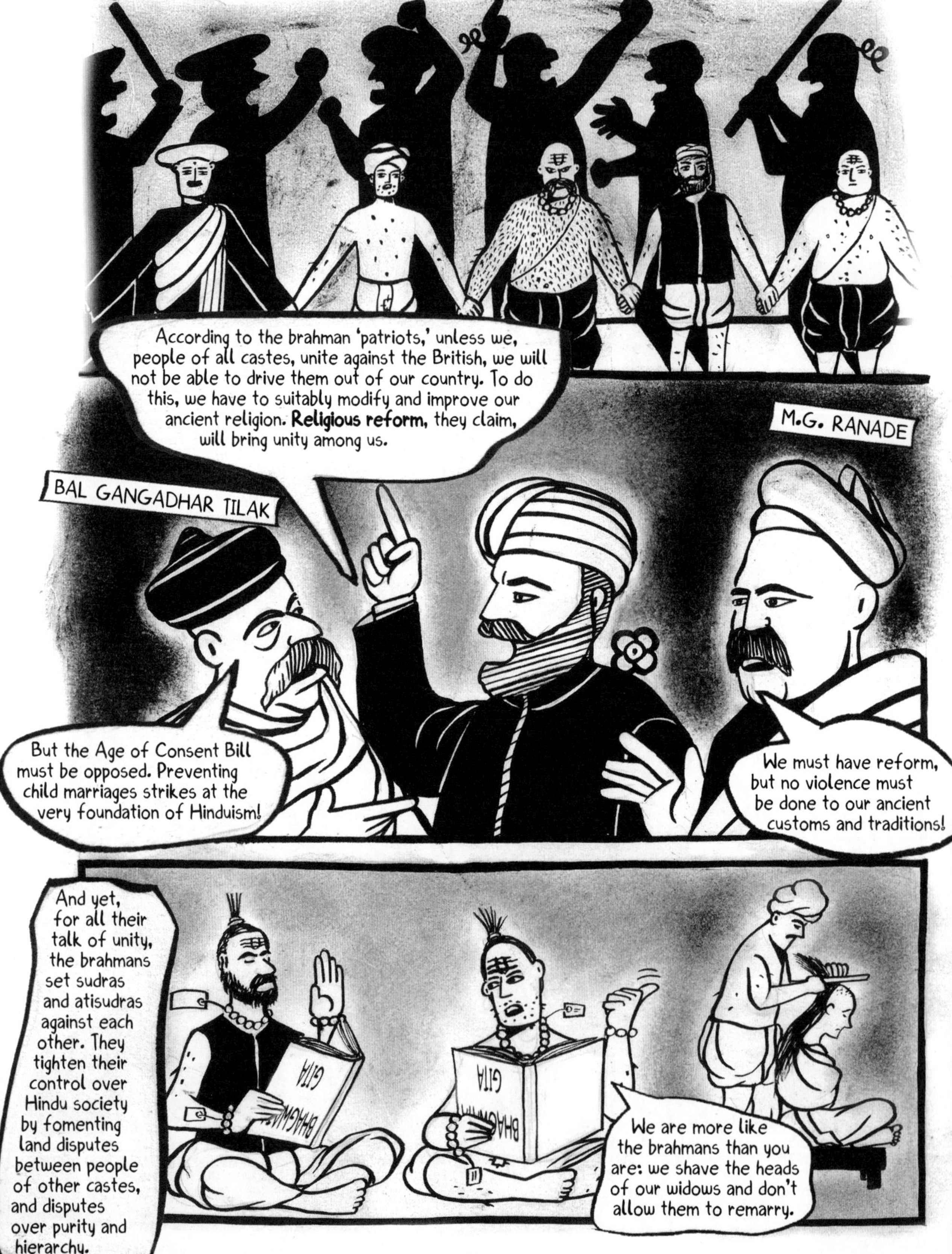

According to the brahman 'patriots,' unless we, people of all castes, unite against the British, we will not be able to drive them out of our country. To do this, we have to suitably modify and improve our ancient religion. **Religious reform**, they claim, will bring unity among us.

M.G. RANADE

BAL GANGADHAR TILAK

But the Age of Consent Bill must be opposed. Preventing child marriages strikes at the very foundation of Hinduism!

We must have reform, but no violence must be done to our ancient customs and traditions!

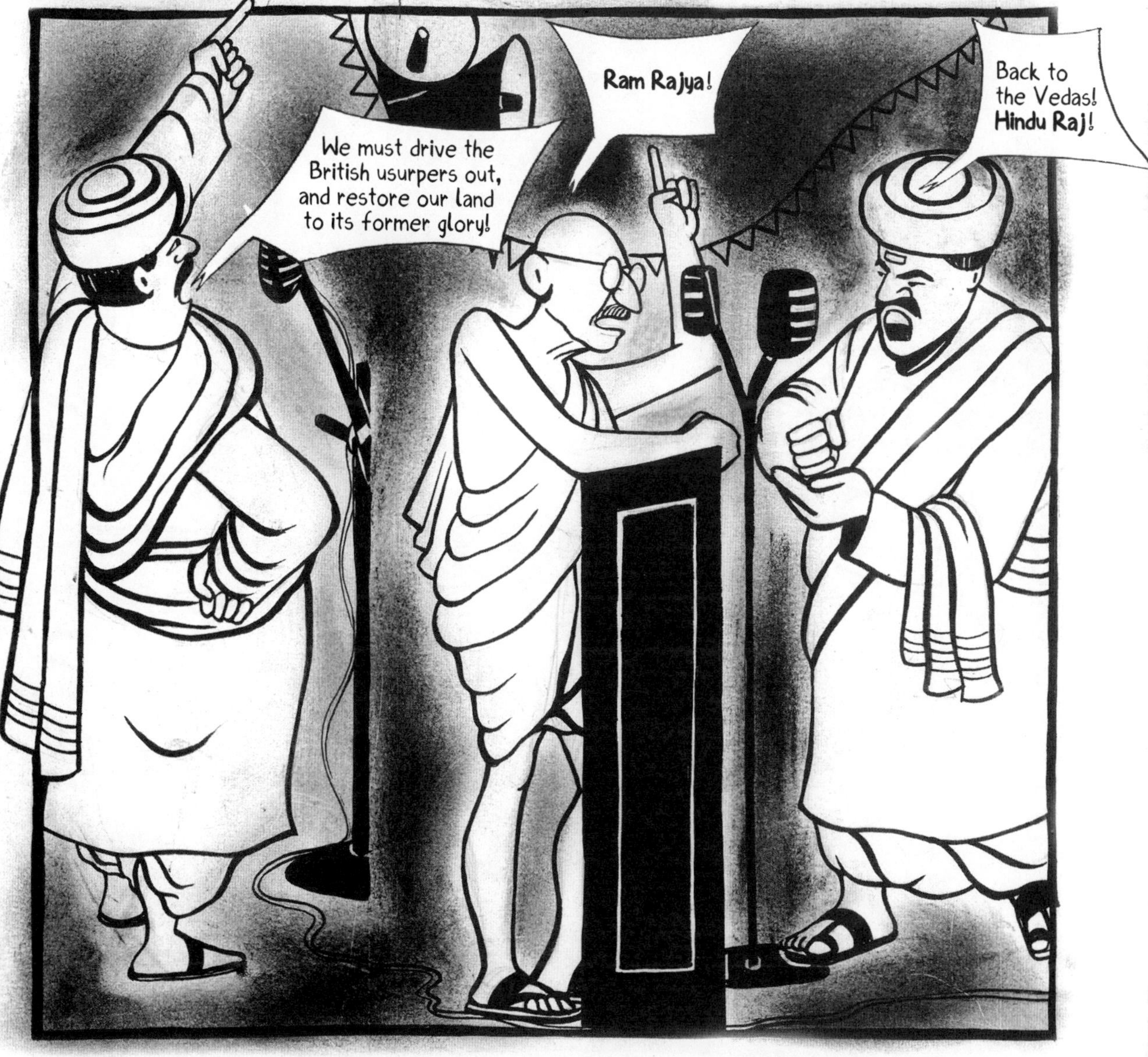

We must drive the British usurpers out, and restore our land to its former glory!

Ram Rajya!

Back to the Vedas! **Hindu Raj!**

These same brahmans who preach unity, and who claim to become clean after drinking the urine of cows, consider clean spring water in the hands of the sudra dirty and undrinkable.

O Hindus! Consolidate and strengthen Hindu nationality!
All those not belonging to the national —the Hindu Race, Religion, Culture and Language— naturally fall out of the pale of real 'National' life.
V.D. SAVARKAR
M.S. GOLWALKAR
Hear, hear!
Shabash!

So how do we strengthen Hindu unity, in a land where, if a sudra's shadow falls on a brahman, or worse still, an atisudra's, the caster of the shadow can be killed?
Even the most liberal of my brahman friends, even those who helped me when I started the schools for atis udra children, started to disagree with me when I began to expose the cunning of their sacred books.
Jotiba, I believe in your mission, but I think you go too far when you criticize our religion!
The critics were not too happy either.
Jotirao's writing is inelegant!
A Sanskrit scholar he is NOT!
What are his sources?
He is just a mouthpiece for the British!
They were taken aback when I suggested that atisudra children should receive a **real** education

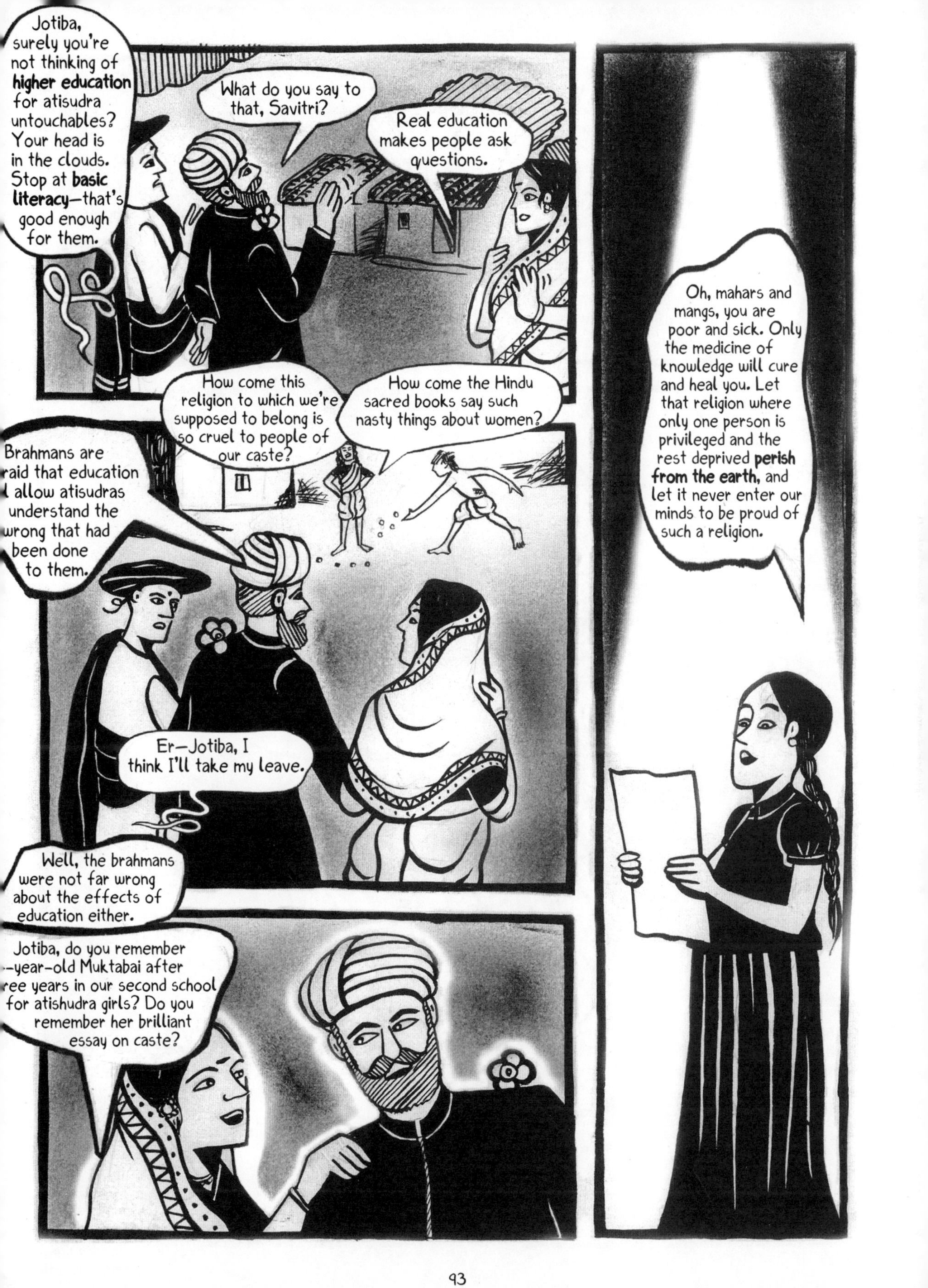

Jotiba, surely you're not thinking of **higher education** for atisudra untouchables? Your head is in the clouds. Stop at **basic literacy**—that's good enough for them.

What do you say to that, Savitri?

Real education makes people ask questions.

How come this religion to which we're supposed to belong is so cruel to people of our caste?

How come the Hindu sacred books say such nasty things about women?

Brahmans are
raid that education
l allow atisudras
understand the
wrong that had
been done
to them.

Er—Jotiba, I think I'll take my leave.

Well, the brahmans were not far wrong about the effects of education either.

Jotiba, do you remember
-year-old Muktabai after
ree years in our second school
for atishudra girls? Do you remember her brilliant essay on caste?

I denounce all the books of the brahmans which decree us their slaves and embrace the book that says all human beings have the right to enjoy human rights in equal measure.

I will not blacken the name of the Creator by allowing anyone to claim, in the name of religion, that some of their fellow human beings are mean and inferior.

And who was in a better place than the author of *Gulamgiri* to stand up for her when Poona society condemned her for her conversion?

Gulamgiri proved to be the manifesto we needed for the Satyashodhak Samaj. I became head of the women's wing, an we set our faces against Hindu practices—the mistreatment of widows, the dependence on brahman priests for the rites of passage, the belief in tyrannical gods. And we women demanded that we be considered equal to men in Hindu society...
The Satyashodak Samaj, Truth-Seekers Society, was founded in Pune on 24 September 1873. It rejected the vedas and brahman supremacy, and encouraged rational thinking.

Vidya, I think I know
what I'm going to buy
oday. This translation
f Tarabai Shinde's
tri-Purush Tulana—A
omparison Between
en and Women. A
rrific example of
rly Indian feminist
olemic.

Tarabai was a member of
the abanshodak Samaj.

I think I'll buy Gail
Omvedt's *Seeking
Begumpura*: the blurb
says it's about the
different ways in which
nonbrahman thinkers
and brahmanical thinkers
imagined utopia. That
sounds fascinating, no?

THE SEEDS OF CHANGE

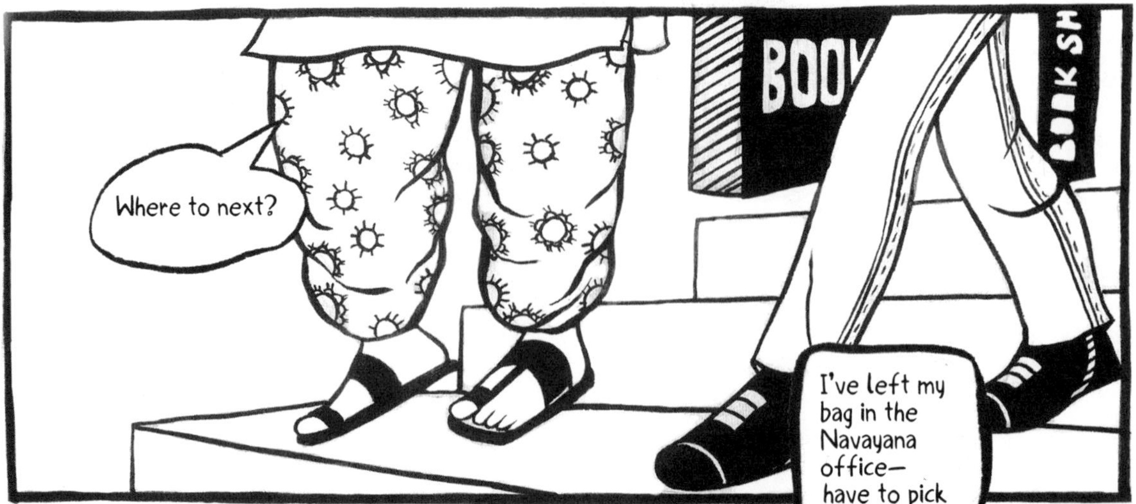

Where to next?

I've left my bag in the Navayana office— have to pick it up. Come with me?

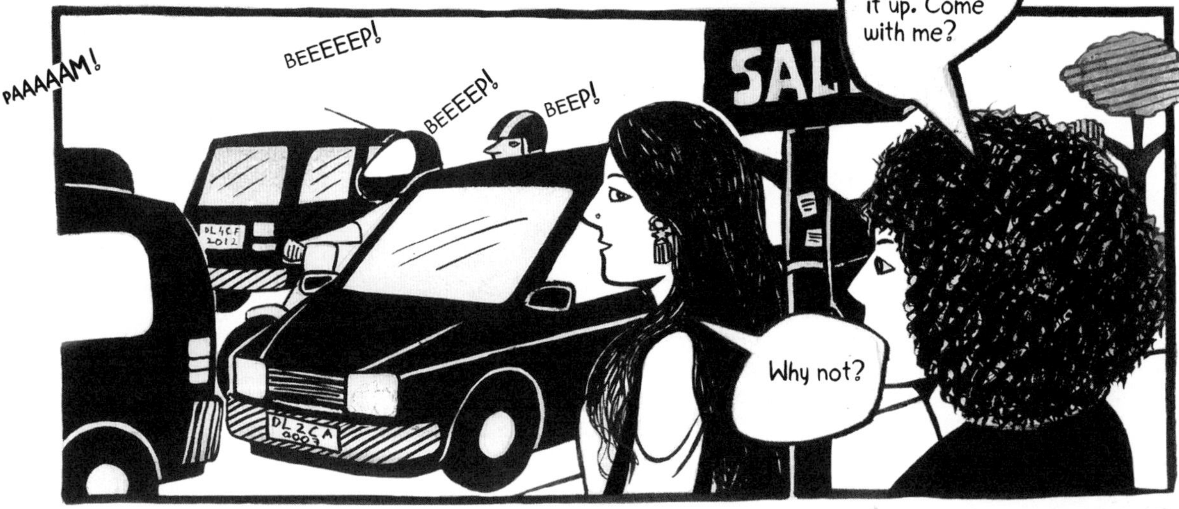

PAAAAAM!

BEEEEEP!

BEEEEP!

BEEP!

Why not?

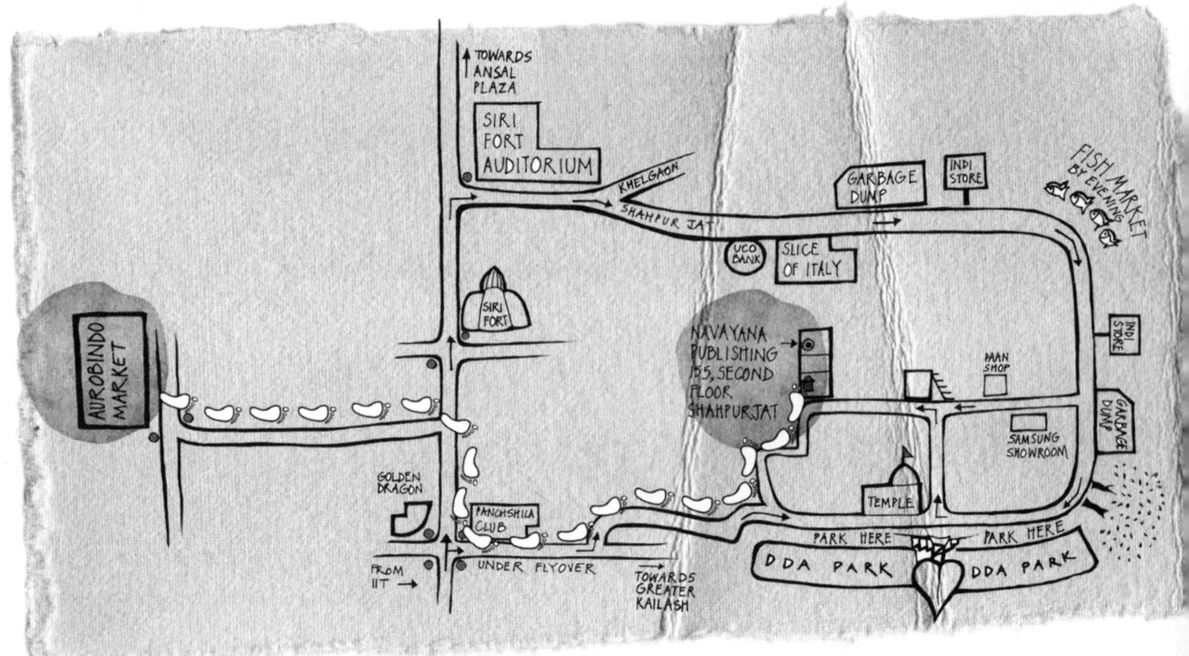

Navayana-Avarna Fellowship
This year, Navayana will sponsor five Dalit/Adivasi candidates at the National Book Trust's four-week Training Course in Book Publishing (in English) in New Delhi. The best professionals from the publishing industry will be teaching the course.
Last date to apply: 10 June 2010.

I'm sure some upper-caste cry-babies are already moaning that these fellowships are only open to dalit candidates.
You know, Appu, my political education began the year the Mandal Commission increased the number of reserved seats in certain jobs for members of Backward castes.
I've read that university campuses erupted in protest all over India. The same thing happened when I was in Stephen's in 2007. I guess this just shows how many students were from brahman or other upper caste backgrounds.
Ban quotas for backward castes or I'll set myself on fire!
DEATH OF MERIT!
IF COBBLERS BECOME DOCTORS WHO WILL MARRY US?
YOUTH FOR EQUALITY
Well, the poor brahmans. They've never gotten over the big comedown—speaking historically —ALL of education and pretty nearly ALL government jobs were, by default, reserved for them in Phule's time.

Jotiba saw Hinduism as fundamentally premised on inequality and on exploitation of 'lower' castes by 'higher' castes, of women by men.
This is why, as he explains to Dhondiba, he rejected Hinduism as the basis of freedom and nationhood.
HINDUISM
NATIONALISM
FREEDOM
Jotiba's emphasis on education and our work together in this field was based on the belief that...

EDUCATION
was the one force that could
LEVEL THE BRAHMANICAL PYRAMID..
HINDUISM

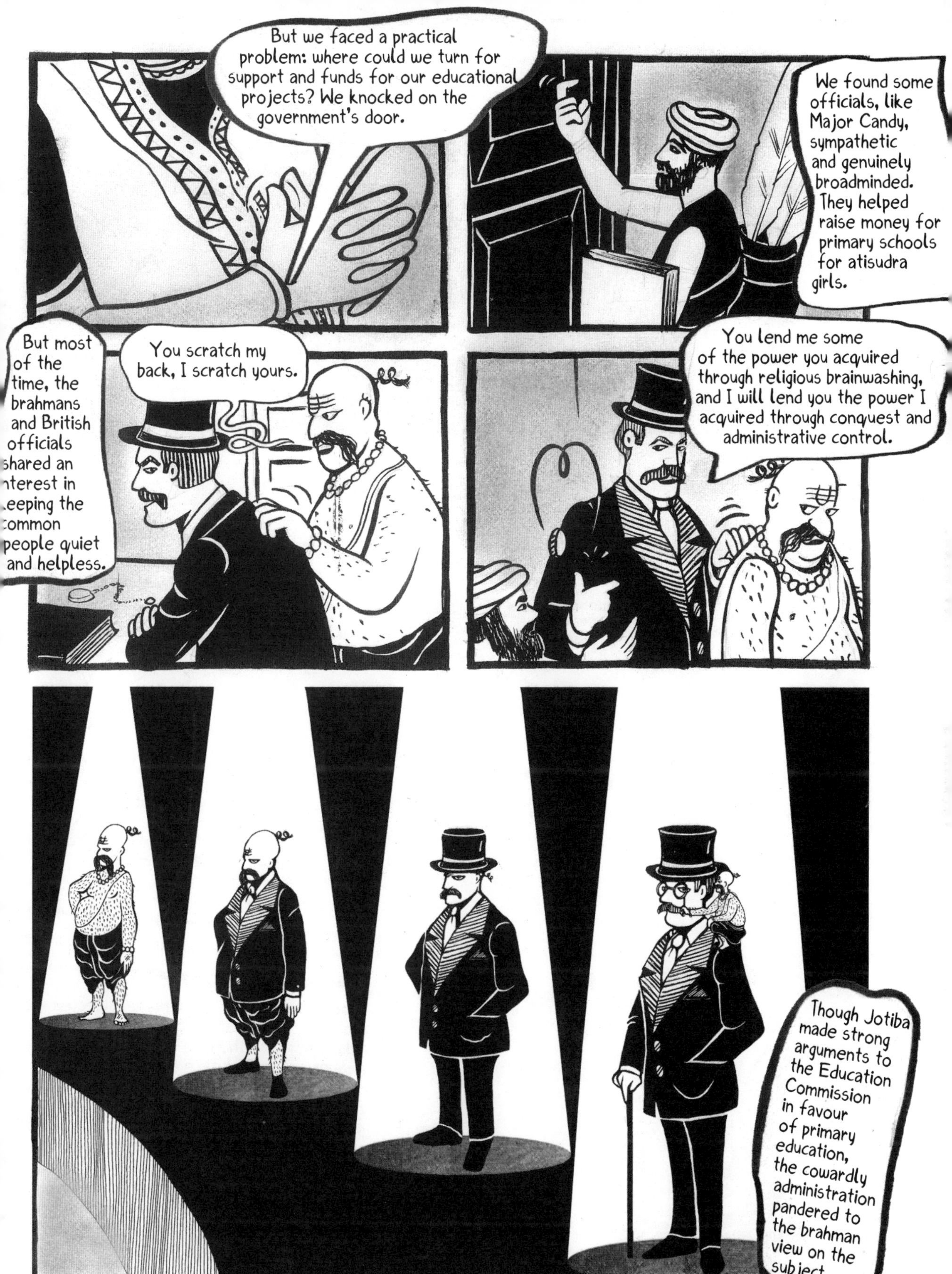

We found some officials, like Major Candy, sympathetic and genuinely broadminded. They helped raise money for primary schools for atisudra girls.

Though Jotiba made strong arguments to the Education Commission in favour of primary education, the cowardly administration pandered to the brahman view on the subject.

JOTIBA'S SPEECH TO THE HUNTER COMMISSION, 1882
The state's revenue is largely collected from peasants. The sweat of the peasant's brow, whic funds higher education, benefits only brahmans. The government must take some of the blame for this. And what contributions have these newly educated sons of wealthy men made to the welfare of their fellow-beings? Have they not kept their knowledge to themselves, not to be soiled by contact with the ignorant vulgar? Meanwhile, education of the masses suffers for want of grants-in-aid.

Jotiba was talking into the wind there. Most of the people in the government were as lazy and self-interested as the brahmans. And since Jotiba didn't think a mere revisionist Hinduism would uproot its evils, he rejected middle-of-the-road groups like the Brahmos and Prarthana Samaji reformers as partners in social revolution.

What is the point of taking such people as partners in change when they can't snatch the razors from the hands of the barbers who shave their young widowed sisters?
What do you need your looks for, now that your man is dead, you miserable bitch?
Your lot now is to serve others!
Thank god we isolate the widows in our family! It is such a high-caste thing to do!

You see, Dhondiba, brahmans—even the reformers among them—wanted sudras, atisudras and women kept forever obedient
They wanted them to have...
no knowledge,
no understanding of religion.
They wanted their own caste united, and this is why they devised the signs by which they would recognize each other:
The sacred thread
and the gayatri-mantra.

They wanted the other castes divided; so they ignited hatred between the sudras and the atisudras.
Silly sudras! if you hate and oppress the atisudras, you will draw closer to us. The more you distance yourselves from atisudras, the higher you will rise in the caste hierarchy.
Don't forget that they foment quarrels against the British! How much worse it will be for the sudras and atisudras if they listen to the brahmans who incite them to rise up against the British!
Yes. When there is rebellion in the name of the heroic god Maruti you can be sure the instigators are brahman, like Tatya Tope, and the followers and supporters sudras, as the Holkars and the Shindes were.
JAI SRI RAM!
MANDIR WAHIN BANAYENGE!
JAI HANUMAN!
Jotiba in fact seems to have anticipated that the hindutva movement would mobilise people in the name of the same monkey god to demolish the Babri mosque...

Dhondiba, you agree with me that the brahmans are lazy and ashamed of manual work?
You mean you want us to **work with our hands**?
They will never weed, plough or sow in the fields; they will never take baskets of manure to the orchard; they will never cut hay and heap it on the haystacks or draw water from the well for the fields.
We'd rather deal in ritual and incantation.
They claim to bring rain or keep away the plague with their black magic and mantras, and fleece the gullible sudras.
The Peshwas handed out dakshina to thousands of brahmans out of money from public taxes. To recognize their learning, apparently. More than half the brahmans who pocketed their money and grew pot-bellied from feasting were shysters and idlers, ignorant as dirt.

Talking of disproportion between the work of one group and another, take the example of a brahman Chief Executive officer in the Education department.

The brahman gets paid Rs 600 a month—Rs 20 a day—to sit in a comfortable chair all day. How many of my kind would it take to earn Rs 7200 a year?
A thousand, labouring incessantly.
The sudra's income depends, too, on the whims and quirks of the brahman whose own income is secure.

So many of these brahmans have wriggled their way into government posts with a little help from their uncles and cousins. Now they infest government offices.
Hey, to get to my boss, you'd better grease this old palm! Do you want your file moved forward or not?
That is because it would be difficult to find even one educated person among the mahars, mangs and chambhars. To find a person with a university education would be next to impossible. The brahmans in government offices are pen-wielding butchers, slitting the throats of the poor—
Why do you say that?

Typical case: the brahman kulkarni catches some illiterate sudra and lends him money.
He writes up mortgage deeds with terrible conditions, impossible to meet. While the deeds are read aloud to the sudra, the conditions are not.
CONTRACT
The brahman clerk suppressed half the document when he read it to me! If only I could have read it myself!

The sudra could complain to the authorities—
But he does not have the skill to write to the Collector to make a complaint. Even if he complained, and the case went before a court, he would have t bribe some brahman to get a hearing.
OUCH!
SPLAT
BZZZZZZZZZ
It is my land, it is all I and my children have!
Stop pestering us, you stupid peasant. Can't you see we're busy here doing sarkari work?
So the villagers say: never leave your house without a lot of grease if you want to get your work done in a government office. Because the brahman middlemen are everywhere, and it is at their pleasure that your petition will go forward.
Do you have the grease power?

If the government were to educate children of all castes, if it selected its officers through examinations, then the government officers could make sure that the illiterate sudras were not swindled and set against each other.
But Jotiba, why doesn't education reach the sudras and atisudras despite the government's efforts?
Because these efforts are not sufficiently radical or far-sighted. Too much government money is devoted to higher education.
Who benefits? Only the brahmans.
We need more **primary** schools.

But even when they open primary schools for sudra children, the teachers, government recruits, are slothful brahmans who despise their charges and constantly worry about being polluted by them.
You—bad boy! Stick your hand really really far out so I can smack it without touching you.

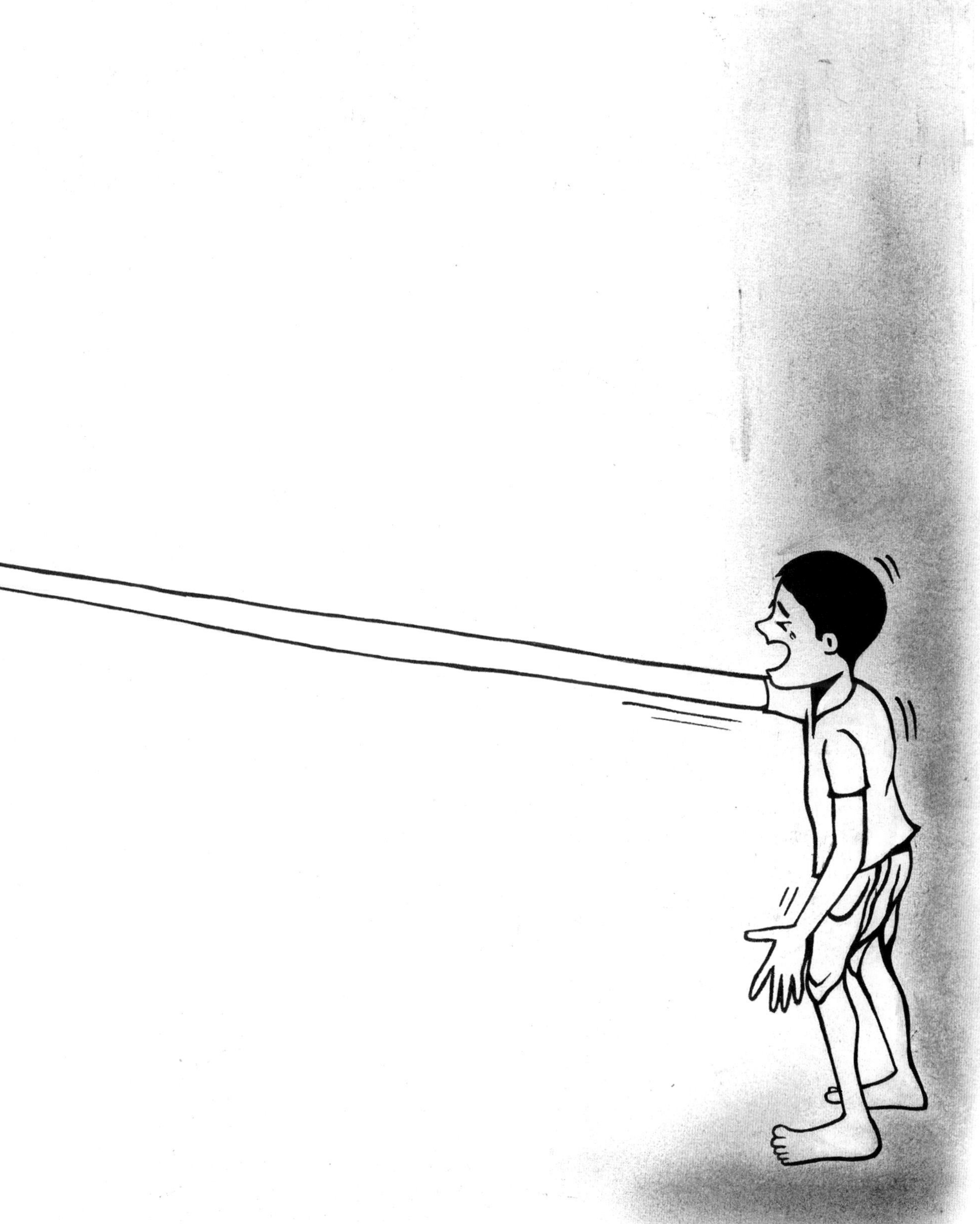

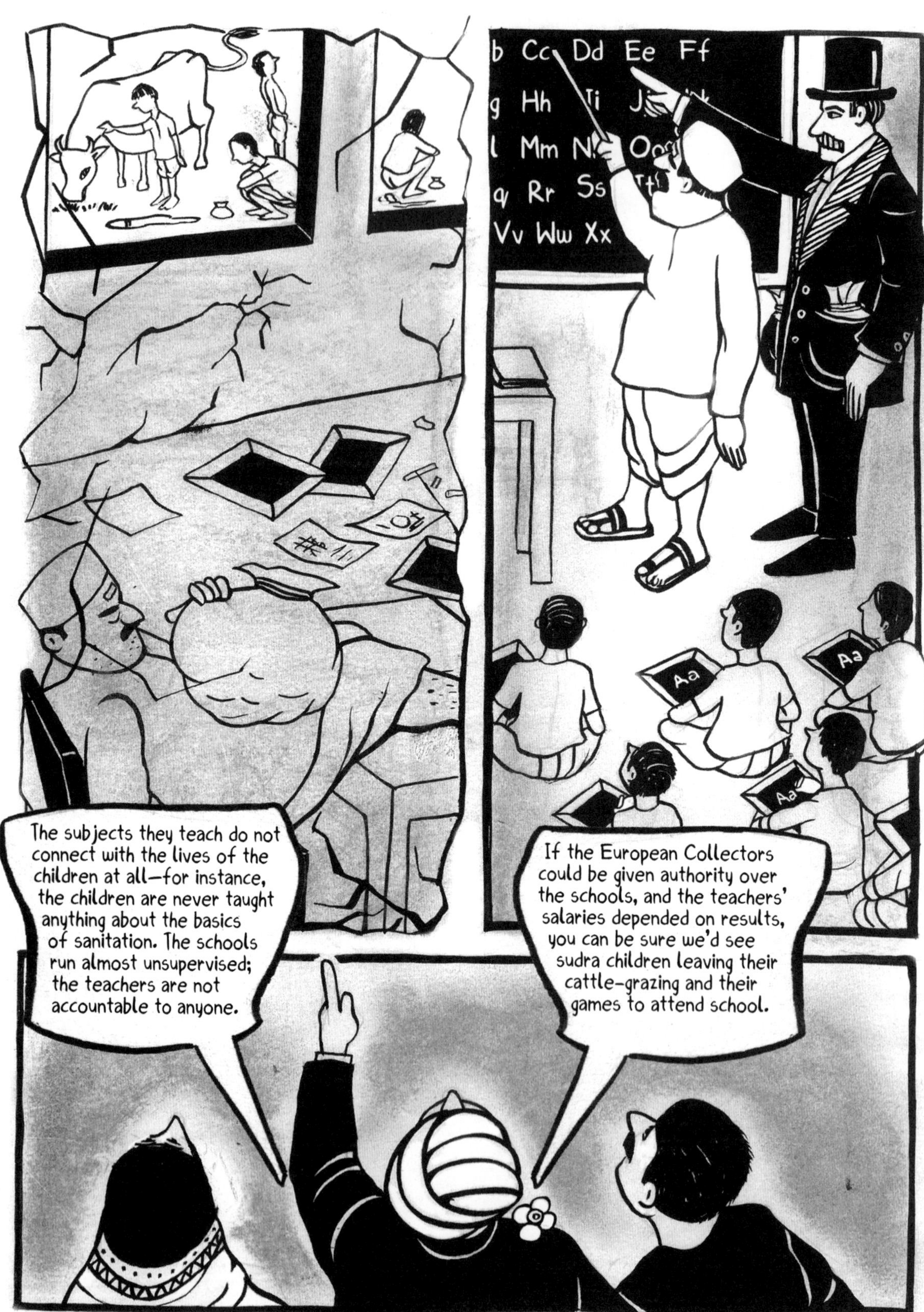
b Cc Dd Ee Ff
g Hh Ii
l Mm
q Rr Ss
Vv Ww Xx
Aa
Aa
Aa
Aa
The subjects they teach do not connect with the lives of the children at all—for instance, the children are never taught anything about the basics of sanitation. The schools run almost unsupervised; the teachers are not accountable to anyone.
If the European Collectors could be given authority over the schools, and the teachers' salaries depended on results, you can be sure we'd see sudra children leaving their cattle-grazing and their games to attend school.

Oh Jotiba, debating the nature of caste with you just makes me mad. I want you to write an article for the newspapers, denouncing the brahmans!
I wrote an article summarizing what we just discussed, Dhondiba, and sent it to several newspapers. Most of them refused to publish it. There's a paragraph in the newspaper lying beside you... read it.
'We have received an article by one Jotirao Govindrao Phule, who considers himself a great scholar, thinker and philosopher, which is full of praise for himself, and defamation of the brahmans. Though a well-known scholar recommends the article, we do not consider the article fit for publication in our journal.'
LOKALYANECCHU
4 JAN 1873
Ah! Well at least you opened my eyes to so many things I never saw before, my friend.
Jotiba and I felt that education could open the third eye.
It could make people refuse to accept what was thrown at them in the name of religion and tradition.
It could make people critical.
It could make women, sudras and atisudras understand how they were being exploited.
It could make people powerful, able to manage their own affairs, invulnerable to scamsters and graft-takers

GO, GET AN EDUCATION!
You've got a golden chance to learn!
So learn and break the chains of caste!
Throw away the brahman's scriptures!
lack of education leads to lack of wisdom, which leads to lack of justice, which leads to lack of progress,
which leads to lack of money, which leads to the oppression of the lower classes. See how lack of education can affect society!

Vidya, listen to this poem by Savitribai. She's such a firebrand! It's called...
RISE TO LEARN AND ACT
My weak and oppressed brothers,
stop living in slavery.
The day of the Manu-worshipping Peshwas is done,
the English, who share knowledge are here.
Learn now. For a millennium you have been denied books.
We will teach our children and ourselves to
seek knowledge; our souls cry out for wholeness,
to leave behind the marks of caste and
unfurl our proud flags in Baliraja's kingdom.
This shall be our war-cry, we shall rise up now,
Rise up now, to learn and to act.

Afterword

THE WRITINGS of Jotirao Phule (1827–1890) filled me with admiration, but if truth be told, it was Savitribai (1831–1897) who lured me in: Phule's child-bride, enigmatic in the scanty accounts of their life, carrying her defiance like a quiet but steady flame. Phule's unusual ability to see that caste oppression, gender inequality, class hierarchies, and racial injustice were deeply interconnected, and his even more radical willingness to make his own household a test case for his belief in human equality: surely some of this was Savitri's doing? So Savitri begins and frames this graphic book on Phule's thought; if she is not a constant presence in these pages, if Dhondiba takes over the role of straight man in Phule's Socratic dialogues, it is because we know so little about her.

This graphic book is a creative writer's and a graphic artist's take on Phule's writings, not a scholarly history of his role in the Indian anticaste movement. Scripting the storyboard, I drew mainly on the *Selected Writings of Jotirao Phule*, edited by G.P. Deshpande. The central text is *Slavery (Gulamgiri)*, but passages from *The Cultivator's Whipcord (Shetkaryacha Asud)* are used to extend some of the ideas touched on in *Slavery*.[1] Since Phule saw a democratized education system as one of the most important solutions to the problems of inequality and exploitation, I also drew on his "Memorial Addressed to the Education Commission". While passages from different texts have sometimes been juxtaposed where they seemed to illuminate each other, and while occasionally the specific words Phule

---

[1] *The Selected Writings of Jotirao Phule*, ed. G.P. Deshpande (New Delhi: LeftWord, 2002). *Slavery* (first published in 1873) is translated in this volume by Maya Pandit; *The Cultivator's Whipcord* (first published in 1883) by Aniket Jaaware.

uses have been slightly modified in the interests of brevity and narrative flow, the ideas, imagery, and often even the tone of Phule's texts, as captured in these translations, have been retained. Dhananjay Keer's *Mahatma Jotirao Phooley: Father of the Indian Social Revolution*[2] provided most of the biographical details. For information on Savitribai, and for her poetry, *A Forgotten Liberator: The Life and Struggles of Savitribai Phule* edited by Braj Ranjan Mani and Pamela Sardar was a useful resource.[3]

When we began working on this project, Aparajita wrote up a list of questions, the answers to which helped us work out a provisional, practical formula for translating Phule's ideas into visual form. For instance: how were we going to blend the historical and the contemporary contexts in terms of the content of Phule's texts and in terms of presentation? Since caste oppression is by no means dead, however much the young urban yuppies wish to believe it is, we wanted to make the point that Phule is relevant today. But since we were inevitably revisiting and reworking both the original text and the context, we marked who we were, without claiming transparency. Aparajita's cheeky postmodern visual presentation of this 'revisiting' gave me much delight as I read the proofs.

To some readers of our draft versions, among the least relevant of Phule's ideas were those related to puranic mythology and cosmology. Why, if we were revisiting the material in his texts, would we want to keep Phule's sometimes serious, sometimes absurd, sometimes positively tedious refutations of puranic origin-myths? Phule's delicious irreverence towards brahmanical Hindu belief systems is, in

[2] Bombay: Popular Prakashan, 1964, rpr 1997.
[3] New Delhi: Mountain Peak, 2008.

and by itself, a good enough justification for retaining his critique: an anti-Hindutva tonic, if nothing else. Why would we want to lose out on the tongue-in-cheek logic that leads Phule to the image of Brahma sulking in polluted seclusion, menstruating through multiple orifices all over his body? Or on the anger with the Peshwa regime—a regime that disguised power-mongering as piety—which leads Phule to dare that "bully," that "audacious ... barbarous villain" Parashuram to return to earth and speak up for his brahman kin?

Phule treats the membrane between history and myth, fantasy and reality, as permeable, to make a point that was crucial to his campaign. The Indo-Aryan origin theories allowed a kind of symbiosis between brahmans and the British colonial overlords with whom they claimed kinship; but logically speaking, Phule argues, if brahman nationalists were protesting against British rule because the British were interlopers, then, as descendants of the Aryans, they were no less interlopers and invaders who seized power from the indigenous people. Phule was all for a transfer of power from colonial governments to indigenous hands; he was also among the first to articulate the fear that if the indigenous hands were those of the comprador brahman middle-class, the transfer would merely consolidate and perhaps extend the forms of caste-based exploitation that already flourished under the British. His emphasis on the education of sudra and atisudra children, both girls and boys, was partly a corollary to this perception: if there were young nonbrahmans educated enough to occupy public office or to contest elections, it would prevent the concentration of power, at all levels, in brahman hands. Thus Phule offered the first edition of *Slavery*—reproduced here in the frontispiece—to general readers at a price of 12 annas, but to "the poor and sudra-atisudras" at a price of 6 annas. *Slavery* was to strengthen the rationalist, anticaste, fiercely egalitarian project of the Satyashodak Samaj (Society of Truthseekers); as historian Rosalind O'Hanlon notes, Satyashodaks even gave away free copies of *Slavery* in villages around Pune in 1874.[4]

In a larger sense, Phule was interested in building a belief system that would be a viable foundation for a liberal, democratic, equitable society. The stranglehold of brahmanical Hinduism had to be loosened through the exposure of its fraudulent, self-serving logic, if such a project was ever to be launched, and if the 'kingdom of Bali'—Phule's trope for a just society, referencing a chain of 'Balirajas' from the mythic Bali himself to Gautama Buddha to Jesus—were to be manifested on earth. Hence the recurrent message—this from a poem by Savitri: "Throw away the brahman's scriptures."

SRIVIDYA NATARAJAN
1 November 2011

[4] *Caste, Conflict and Ideology: Mahatma Jotirao Phule and Low Caste Protest in Nineteenth Century Maharashtra* (Cambridge: Cambridge University Press, 1985).